THE T

DONALD J. D. MULKERNE received his B.S. and Ed.M. degrees from Boston University and his Ed.D. from Columbia University. He has taught at Rockland (Massachusetts) High School, Catholic University of America, Boston University, Russell Sage College, College of St. Rose, and since 1950 at State University of New York at Albany.

He is the author of eight texts and reference books and more than twenty articles and research papers. Dr. Mulkerne has been the principal speaker at more than 100 high school commencement exercises, teachers' conventions and at management and service club meetings. He conducts many workshops on written and oral communications.

DONALD J. D. MULKERNE, JR., received his B.A. from Plattsburgh State University College, New York, his M.Ed. degree from Bowling Green State University, Ohio, and his Ph.D. from the University of Florida at Gainesville. He has taught at Sante Fe Community College, has been a counselor in the Alachua County Public School system, Gainesville, and was in private practice as a psychologist.

He currently is with the State of Alabama, Department of Mental Health, Division of Mental Retardation, as a psychologist. Dr. Mulkerne has written numerous articles that have appeared in professional journals and has been a speaker at workshops and conventions.

THE TERM PAPER
Step by Step

DONALD J. D. MULKERNE, ED.D.

DONALD J. D. MULKERNE, JR., PH.D.

Anchor Books
ANCHOR PRESS/DOUBLEDAY
GARDEN CITY, NEW YORK

Library of Congress Cataloging in Publication Data
Mulkerne, Donald J. D.
    The term paper.
    Includes index.
    1. Report writing—Handbooks, manuals, etc.
I. Mulkerne, Donald J. D., 1951– . II. Title.
LB2369.M84   1983   808′.02   82–45487
       ISBN: 0-385-18231-7

CONTENTS

CHAPTER 1 Introduction 1

CHAPTER 2 Choosing and Limiting the Subject 6

CHAPTER 3 Using the Library 12

CHAPTER 4 Preparing the Bibliography 39

CHAPTER 5 Taking Notes 44

CHAPTER 6 Making the Outline 49

CHAPTER 7 Writing the Paper 55

CHAPTER 8 Footnoting 61

CHAPTER 9 Typing the Paper 69

CHAPTER 10 Developing the Oral Report 76

Oral Report Checklist 95

A Sample Term Paper: Lincoln's
Assassination—A Murder Mystery 99

Term Paper Checklist 117

Abbreviations Commonly Used in
Reference Books 119

Index 123

THE TERM PAPER

THE LERM PAPER

CHAPTER 1

INTRODUCTION

THE PURPOSE OF THIS MANUAL

This book is designed to help you write your term paper—indeed any research paper for which you must plan carefully to find, organize, and present information from a number of sources—whether this paper is your first or your twentieth.

It is a basic source of reference which will:

Help you choose a subject.

Show you how to get the most out of library resources.

Explain the purpose of the bibliography and footnotes as well as the mechanics of presenting them.

Suggest notetaking techniques.

Guide you in developing an outline.

Assist you in writing a paper from your outline so it will be prepared in acceptable style.

Show you how to set up simple tables.

Provide you with step-by-step procedures for typing the final copy from your draft in the proper form.

Include a finished term paper to illustrate the various procedures covered in this manual.

In addition to helping you write your term paper, Chapter 10 has a very complete listing of ideas on how to prepare and give an oral report.

WHY WRITE TERM PAPERS?

Why do college students have to prepare term papers? Skills in English usage and experience in expressing ideas on paper in a readable and interesting manner can be acquired by writing original expository themes. The preparation of a research paper, however, offers further challenges to you. It demands that you use your library skills to gather, interpret, and report on facts and ideas impartially, honestly, and clearly.

Preparing a term paper will:

> Give you experience in locating information quickly and choosing among available sources as well as acquainting you with the library resources from which information can be drawn.
>
> Give you a broad and thorough grasp of the subject area you have researched.
>
> Teach you selectivity, for you will do much more reading than writing for your paper. You must not only choose from your reading what should be included in your paper, but also judge the relative importance of that information to your context.
>
> Develop your writing skills and vocabulary so you can communicate more effectively.

WHAT THE TERM PAPER IS NOT

The term paper is not a thesis or a dissertation. These two graduate papers go much more deeply into a particular subject and require a great deal of time, effort, research, and an extensive bibliography. In many cases, statistical interpretations are made. The term paper is less formal, shorter, shows evidence of some reading background, contains a bibliography and rarely makes use of statistical procedures or includes graphs and charts.

However, the term paper is not a popular novel. It should keep to facts, treat *pro* and *con* data fairly, and present its evidence in a scholarly manner that is interesting to read.

Neither is a term paper a mere listing of what several sources have to say about its topic. This kind of writing is lifeless, boring, and adds nothing to the knowledge already available on the subject. A worthwhile paper has form, its own introduction and conclusions.

Finally, a term paper is not:

> A pseudoscholarly collection of footnotes which require the reader to break his or her span of concentration by shifting

the eyes back and forth from context to footnote to context.

A summary of one book or of what one person has to say about your topic.

A carelessly written composition containing many errors of grammar, logic, mechanics, and omissions of facts.

An attempt at original research of the laboratory-experimentation type commonly employed in doctoral dissertations.

WHAT THE TERM PAPER IS

Your term paper should be an unbiased account of a topic documented with pertinent and valid information in support of whatever statements you make.

Your paper may be of the argumentative or of the storytelling type. The argumentative paper attempts to prove that something is right or wrong, good or bad, desirable or undesirable. The storytelling type surveys a subject by drawing upon pertinent references bearing upon a particular point, and then is written about the highlights of what has been read, without attempting to prove or disprove anything. The sample paper illustrated at the end of this manual is of the storytelling type.

Documentation—the use of quotations—is a distinguishing feature of term papers. Each quotation must carry a footnote which identifies its source since it is important in this type of paper to know who said what. These quotations must be carefully selected and used only when really necessary to bring out a point you are trying to make. Too many quotations make for a choppy paper, and your instructor will note that he or she is reading what many other people think rather than what you think as illustrated by your choice of quotations. Failure to identify quoted matter and passing it off as one's own is *dishonest* and may well result in a failing mark.

The term paper, while its content is drawn from numerous sources, has the style of a well-written composition. Simply expressed, your paper will contain a short statement of its purpose, followed by your evidence presented in a logical manner and arranged for smooth reading. The paper will be completed with a few appropriate remarks which summarize the highlights of your research. Any conclusions you draw must be based upon your evidence.

Furthermore, the language of the paper will be related to its purpose. Are you trying to persuade, explain, relate, or entertain? Once you have decided this, you will know the degree of formality your paper should assume and the kind of vocabulary you should use. Using big words having many syllables without fully understanding their meaning may result in wrong word choices. Avoid trying to lengthen your paper by adding extra words just to reach a minimum set by your instructor. Conciseness, rather than wordiness, and simplicity, rather than floweriness, should be your stylistic goals.

Finally, the term paper reflects you and the quality of your thinking. It should be factual and at the same time fair, including all evidence you find in your readings even though some of it may weaken your original position about your subject. Remember that progress is also made by discovering that what you once thought to be true is, in fact, false. What would you think of a pharmaceutical firm that put a drug on the market, guaranteed it to cure the common cold but failed to inform the public that severe headaches would result from its use? It is just as dishonest to mislead your reader by failing to include evidence contrary to your viewpoint and in so doing commit a serious error of omission. Such "slanting" is not likely to go unnoticed.

The most difficult job in writing is to get started. Begin where it is easiest for you: sit down and write all you now know about your subject—if you have one. If you have yet to select a subject, turn to Chapter 2.

How Is This Book to Be Used?

This manual provides key ideas to show you—as closely as any book can—exactly how to go about writing your paper. These key ideas are expressed in short simple sentences, each of which is numbered consecutively by chapter. Thus, beginning with Chapter 2, suggestions for writing an effective term paper appear as numbered items such as 2.1, 2.2, and so forth. In many instances, these numbers have been noted on the sample term paper at the end of the book. For example, look in Chapter 5 and locate 5.27. Read the item. Note that an example is provided in the term paper, page 3. Turn to that page in the term paper and you will find **5.27.** This coding system enables you to easily look up the explanation or the reason for the use of a particular form.

Some users of this book prefer to read Chapter 1 and then go directly to the sample term paper and read it carefully, paying special attention to all items in bold face. Each of these refers them back to a particular chapter in the book. For example, **5.27** refers to Chapter 5, item 27 or 5.27. Then with that introduction of reading the term paper, they go back to Chapter 2 and proceed through the book systematically.

CHAPTER 2

CHOOSING AND LIMITING THE SUBJECT

Choosing a subject is deceptively difficult and should not be treated lightly. While it may seem to require less physical effort than the other parts of preparing a paper, deciding on an appropriate subject and limiting it to a degree where you can give it the attention it needs will in the long run result in a completed paper of which you can be proud. Don't jump into choosing a topic. Selecting a topic impulsively or intuitively may cause you to regret your haste, for your paper may later bog down to a discouraging halt. Reflect upon each of the following suggestions, for they will help you get off to a good start.

2.1. Understand your assignment.

Listen to your instructor as he or she describes your term paper assignment. Understand its purpose, the length of the paper, the due date, the limits within which you must confine your subject, the type of paper you are to prepare—argumentative or storytelling. Keep your instructor's comments on file and refer to them frequently.

2.2. Your subject may be assigned, you may choose your own, or you may choose a subject within a certain area defined by your instructor.

If your instructor assigns you a subject, your task is simplified because you are now ready to make your plans for collecting the data. If you must choose your own subject, read items 2.3 through 2.17. If your subject must be confined within a certain area, such as English, History, or Geology, examine book and periodical indexes for ideas. Read Chapter 3 of this manual and then if you have questions, consult with your college, school, or local librarian.

2.3. Think about your assignment and if your instructor has invited discussion, go to him or her with your ideas.

Develop a tentative plan of attack by listing reference books, indexes, periodicals, and other aids which may be of assistance to you. If term papers are on file for student examination, read several of them. Make a list of questions to ask your instructor. You are now ready for your initial interview with him or her.

2.4. The title of your subject may be in the form of a question or a positive statement.

Subjects for term papers expressed in question form:

Of What Value Are Term Papers to College Students?

What Are the Requisites for Success in Business?

What Can Be Done to Help Reduce Water Pollution and Acid Rain?

What Compelled Booth to Kill Lincoln?

Subjects for term papers expressed as positive statements:

The Influence of Unions on the Safety of Workers

Color and Lighting for Office Illumination

A Suggested Plan for Utilizing Television as a Learning Aid

Booth and His Motives for Killing Lincoln

2.5. Select a subject in line with the basic purposes of your course.

If you are completing a term paper for an English course, consider the advisability of writing about a subject in the English area. Determine the purpose of your term paper. Consider the reason that motivated your instructor to request such an assignment from you. As a result of writing your paper, are you supposed to be a better writer, a better thinker, a better researcher, or better informed about your subject? Knowing the reason for your assignment will help you write a paper in keeping with the requirements of your course.

2.6. Select a subject in which you have a strong interest, curiosity, experience, or competency.

When interest and curiosity are present, your writing task becomes a delightful experience rather than a chore. Prior experience and competency in your subject reduce the danger of making unwise statements in your paper or failing to report the basic facts.

2.7. Select a subject in which information is readily available.

The subject should not be so new that information is difficult to obtain. Generally speaking, your school or college library or the local library should be well equipped, so that you can do all your reading in the local area. Consult your librarian and ask his or her opinion about the availability of data on your chosen subject. Choose a subject in which adequate and reliable information is available.

Examples of subjects having limited or unreliable data:

Aircraft Stations in Outer Space

U.S.A.—A.D. 3000

The Inside Story of Security Measures Taken at the John F. Kennedy Space Center

Booth's Private Conversations with His Conspirators

The Secret Thoughts of John Wilkes Booth

The Genealogy of the Conspirators of Lincoln

2.8. Select a subject with your audience in mind.

Consider that another human being will read your paper. If you know the viewpoint and the interest level of your instructor about your chosen subject, your paper will be more to the point and more interesting for him or her to read. If you know how informed your reader already is about your topic, it will be to your advantage to write a paper that goes beyond the reader's present range of knowledge. The reader should learn something by reading your paper.

2.9. Select a subject important enough to warrant your attention, and if possible, one that correlates with other courses you are taking. In so doing you will then work with information that will help you improve in history or whatever.

Choose a subject that is intellectually respectable, offers practical value, and is capable of being developed fully into a thesis or a dissertation at some future time.

Examples of subjects lacking intellectual respectability or practical value:

Penguins of the South Pole (for a non-zoologist and a paper which has a travelogue flavor)

Fun at a Fair

The Manufacture of Christmas Candles

The Pizza Pie

2.10. Select a subject that can be researched within the time limits set by your instructor.

Determine how much time you have to complete your paper. Set deadlines for each phase of your research and writing task. Don't take on too ambitious a topic. Choose a broad subject area and then limit it.

Examples of subjects too ambitious for term papers:

Lincoln: The Full Story of the Assassination and Trial

The Rise and Fall of the Roman Empire

The Conquests of Napoleon

The World's Great Musicians

U.S. Presidents

The above topics might be used if they cover a smaller area:

Lincoln—the Last Year of His Life

The Rise of the Roman Empire

Napoleon Wins a Battle

American Composers of Jazz in the 1920s

U.S. Presidents of the Twentieth Century

2.11. Select a subject that is not too narrow.

Examples of subjects that are too narrow:

Hazardous Waste Damage in Lake Erie for August 1983

> Diseases of Fleas
> High School Economics for First-semester Seniors in Alaska
> Lincoln—His Service as a Postmaster

2.12. Select a subject that does not involve technical information beyond your comprehension.

> Examples of subjects that might be too technical:
> The Thermonuclear Bomb Ingredients
> Drugs for Arthritis
> Xerography—How It Works
> Flights of Trajectories and Their Geometric Patterns

2.13. Select a subject suitable for student investigation and in good taste. A sensational subject appears more often to be a childish choice rather than a clever one. Someone is going to read your paper—make his or her time worthwhile.

> Examples of subjects not in good taste:
> The Heroic Qualities of Dillinger
> A Positive Look at Hedonism
> Earning a Living by Gambling

2.14. Select a subject that is not too neutral.

> Examples of subjects too neutral:
> Insurance Mortality Tables
> Filing Cases
> Advantages of Electricity over Gaslight

2.15. Select a subject that is clear.

> Examples of subjects that may not be clear:
> Quakers and Friends
> Running for the Office
> Banks

2.16. Select a subject that does not have a universal acceptance.

> Examples of subjects that have universal acceptance:
> Pollution Control Laws are Needed
> AA—Does It Serve a Useful Purpose?
> Did John Wilkes Booth Kill Lincoln?

2.17. If none of the suggestions in Nos. 2.3 to 2.16 help, and you are still searching for an idea for a paper, turn to Chapter 3 and pay particular attention to Nos. 3.44(a) to (v). An idea for a topic might come to mind merely by reading titles and content coverage of books and periodicals.

CHAPTER 3

USING THE LIBRARY

Libraries have become very sophisticated in recent years and have added many features and services to the science of storing and finding data and information. While most libraries still use the word *library* to identify their function, other terms may be used such as *Information Science Center* and *Information Resources Center*. The word *library* is used throughout this manual because it is the more common term.

The library is an educational tool. To get the greatest benefit from it, you must use it wisely. When you consider how often you will need the services of the library, you can appreciate the value of becoming skilled in library procedure. The benefits to be gained from wise use of the library facilities are numerous, but two override all others: pertinent references are easily located and time is saved when you "know your way around" in the library.

3.1. Most libraries prepare a set of instructions on how to use the facilities most effectively. Obtain a copy from the main desk or in the lobby and study it. Do this in advance of your actual research in the library.

3.2. Material found in the library usually is of three types:
general information
reference materials
periodicals

3.3. Most books "on reserve" must remain in the library during the day and are charged out only with permission at night, weekends, and holidays.

3.4. A Circulation or Loan Department charges out books (except those on reserve) for approximately two weeks.

3.5. Government publications and periodicals are usually not charged out but may be loaned for use in the Reading Room.

3.6. The Reference Librarian is a specialist in locating information and is available to help you when help is needed, or at any other time.

3.7. The Reference Room contains encyclopedias, handbooks, magazines, newspapers, and dictionaries of various types. Materials in this room are not available for overnight use.

3.8. The Periodicals Department is where you will find current newspapers and magazines. Usually, these materials are not available on a loan basis.

3.9. Many libraries have *divisional* reading rooms where books, periodicals, and other printed and audiovisual materials are gathered in special areas and grouped by subject matter. Such divisions often include Humanities, Social Studies, Sciences, Government Publications, Record Collection, and Newspapers. You may want to visit a *divisional* reading room to collect data for your paper.

3.10. An interlibrary loan service may be available whereby you may be able to borrow books, other printed matter, microfilms, and other audiovisuals for a modest charge. However, such service is usually slow—perhaps even weeks before you receive what you have requested. Allow enough time in your research plan in case you need to use this interlibrary loan service.

3.11. The library may have an Information Retrieval Section which can prepare computer-produced bibliographies using the ERIC, MEDLARS, *Psychological Abstracts,* and *Biological Abstracts* data bases. It may edit and distribute manually produced bibliographies and library guides.

3.12. Some university libraries are able to search by computer for information on many topics. References to journal articles, books, research reports, and other types of materials have been combined to form databases, many of which correspond to printed indexes and abstracts covering a broad range of disciplines.

3.13. The result of a computer search is a bibliography or listing of citations to journal articles, serials, monographs, government publications, etc., related to your topic. Each citation includes full bibliographic information to help you locate items identified by the search. In some cases, abstracts or short summaries of the citations may also be printed if you request them. *Not all libraries are equipped to conduct computer searches.*

3.14. Consult your librarian to determine if a computer search is part of the library's service. If it is, the usual procedure is to complete a search request, defining your problem carefully in a concise narrative statement. Also, arrange for an appointment with the librarian who is trained to search the database(s) you need. During your appointment, your request will be reviewed with you by the librarian, who, with your assistance, will formulate a search strategy.

3.15. (a) For example, ERIC is your major source for locating information on education topics. You need to become familiar with ERIC terminology in order to do your search. Using the *Thesaurus of ERIC Descriptors,* identify key descriptors (subject terms) relevant to your search, such as "Grading." You might also want to expand your search to include some of the narrower terms (NT), broader terms (BT), or related terms (RT) listed under the descriptor heading as shown in the example below.

SN (scope note) denotes a term's usage in ERIC. UF (used for) is a cross-reference and should *not* be used for your search.

GRADING   *Jul. 1966*
    CIJE: 716   RIE: 499
SN   Process of rating an individual's or group's performance, achievement, or less frequently, behavior, using specifically established scales of values
UF   Contract Grading ※ Marking (Scholastic)

NT Credit No Credit Grading
    Pass Fail Grading
BT Achievement Rating
RT Academic Achievement
    Educational Testing
    Grade Inflation
    Grade Prediction
    Grades (Scholastic)
    Informal Assessment
    Report Cards
    Scoring
    Student Evaluation
    Student Teacher Relationship
    Summative Evaluation

(b) Consult the monthly issues of *Resources in Education* (RIE). Check the Subject Index sections under the descriptor "Grading" and other applicable descriptors you have chosen to identify *titles* of current documents on the subject.

Check the semiannual and annual indexes to *Resources in Education* for relevant documents using the same descriptors.

Grade 8
Report on the Intermediate Evaluation Project.
ED 164 622
Report on the Intermediate Evaluation Project-Phase II.
ED 164 588
Grading
Institutional Research, Fiscal Year 1977: Perceptions of Mastery Grading. Research Monograph VIII.
ED 164 061

Each document is identified by an accession number (ED plus six digits).

(c) Extend your search to the periodical literature by consulting the monthly indexes of *Current Index to Journals in Education* (CIJE).

Check the monthly, semiannual, and annual subject indexes of *Current Index to Journals in Education,* using the same descriptors.

Grading

A Contractual Examination: Another Alternative, *College English* v39 n3, pp368-70,   Nov 77
EJ 169 448

"Sign Now, Pay Later": Further Experiments in Student Grading, *Exercise Exchange* v21 n1, pp9-12,   F 76   EJ 169 477

Reporting Pupil Progress in Reading—Parents vs. Teachers, *Reading Teacher* v31 n3, pp294-6, Dec 77   EJ 169 510

Computer-Graded Homework in Introductory Physics, *American Journal of Physics* v45 n10, pp896-8,   Oct 77   EJ 170 425

An Alternative Scoring Formula for Multiple-Choice and True-False Tests, *Journal of Educational Research* v70 n6, pp335-9, Jul/Aug 77   EJ 170 686

The identifying numbers for journal articles in CIJE are labeled EJ.

(d) From the Subject Indexes, go to the Document Résumé section of RIE or the Main Entry section of CIJE to read the abstract of the document or journal article. These sections are clearly marked, and the identifying numbers (ED or EJ) are listed consecutively. You can then determine whether you want to obtain the full text of the document or article. Availability information is given in each résumé.

EJ 169 477   CS 710 521
"Sign Now, Pay Later": Further Experiments in Student Grading Klein, Julie Thompson, *Exercise Exchange,* v21 n1, pp9-12, F 76
*English Instruction, *Grading, *Teaching Techniques, *Contracts, Secondary Education, Higher Education
Presents an eight-point plan, with illustrations, for assigning student grades. (JM)
Reprint Available (See p. vii): UMI

Locate the journal articles (EJ accession numbers) in your library, or consult the introduction to CIJE for reprint ordering information.

(e) Notice how a full description of the title, source, publication date, number of pages, price, descriptors, and a summary of the research article is shown.

ED 164 061   JC 790 070
Institutional Research, Fiscal Year 1977: Percep-
tions of Mastery Grading. Research Monograph
VIII.
South Oklahoma City Junior Coll., Okla.
Pub Date—77
Note—53p.
EDRS Price MF-$0.83 HC-$3.50 Plus Postage.
Descriptors—*Academic Records, Administrator
   Attitudes, *Attitudes, Community Colleges,
   Counselor Attitudes, Employer Attitudes, Grades
   (Scholastic), *Grading, Higher Education, Insti-
   tutional Research, *Junior Colleges, *Mastery
   Learning, School Funds, Secondary Education,
   Student Attitudes, Student Evaluation, Student
   Financial Aid, *Surveys, Teacher Attitudes,
   Transfer Policy, Transfer Students
   The grading policy at South Oklahoma City Junior College (SOCJC) allows a student to master a
course by doing a specified amount of work to a
pre-determined standard (80% mastery). When this
is accomplished, the student receives an "M" indicating mastery; otherwise, nothing appears on the
official record. No A, B, C, grades are awarded. This
document compiles six studies dealing with the perceptions of the "M" grade by different SOCJC con-
stituencies. The first survey examined employers of
the college's students. Employers preferred a traditional transcript though about two-thirds would accept a list of student competencies. Next studied
were other institutions of higher education, which
also preferred transcripts allowing student compari-
sons; however, no SOCJC students had been denied
entrance to these transfer schools. A third study of
financial aid offices examined effects on both student aid at transfer institutions as well as on
SOCJC's ability to obtain student aid funds. It appeared students may have had trouble getting schol-
arships, though the college itself had no problem
getting funds. A need was seen for added information and explanation about the system in the next
survey of high school counselors. The fifth survey
concerned student attitudes. About 40-45% saw the
"M" as an advantage, while 23-30% saw it as a
disadvantage. The final report studied faculty and
staff perceptions. The majority felt the system was
an advantage to students but the problems in trans-
ferring and the fact that there is no reward for ex-
cellence were disadvantages. (MB)

3.16. The Microfilm Department, if your library has one, has reduced thousands of printed and written matter to microscopic size. Film copies of the New York *Times* and other major newspapers are usually available for viewing on special machines that magnify the print.

Microcard, microcopy, microfiche, microfilm, and microprint refer to the manner in which data are stored. The generic word for this is *microform* which is a process of reproducing printed and written matter in a much-reduced size. Some type of film reader is required. A Microform Room stores newspapers, periodicals, and books on microfilm, microfiche, and microcards.

While only the most modern libraries have all this equipment, there is a good chance that *some* of it is available. Check with the librarian.

3.17. Automation is becoming more and more important and visible in library services. Long Distance Xerography (referred to as LDX) where available, allows you to get Xerox copies of printed matter in minutes. However, this service is currently available only to librarians rather than to library users.

3.18. Many libraries have copying machines such as Xerox. A modest fee is charged for their use. Rather than copying a page from a book, you might want to make a Xerox copy of it as this will save you writing time. A microprinter may also be available.

3.19. Librarians are available to answer intelligent questions— even questions that are not clearly thought out. Understand clearly the nature of your problem before asking for help. But if you need help, your librarian is waiting to assist you.

3.20. If you have a "dial access" system in the library, you may be able to get special and unusual help from a master computer console. This console stores great quantities of data and information. Ask your librarian for help.

3.21. Many libraries have audiovisual equipment available for use in the library including movie projectors, overhead projectors, tape recorders, record players, slide and film-strip projectors. A Learning Resources Center, if one is available, usually includes the Curriculum Library Collection, non-print media, and the phonograph record collection. Record players and earphones are usually available.

3.22. If the library is equipped with electronic carrels, ask your librarian for assistance. Typical carrels are equipped with TV, earphones, radios, motion picture projectors, and screen, slide viewers, typewriters, and other A-V aids.

3.23. If the library has a Special Collections Section, it will probably contain materials that require special treatment such as manuscripts, rare books, reprint series, and specialized subject collections.

3.24. Rotary files have inserts with typed or printed headings listing the periodicals subscribed to and available in the Periodical Room.

3.25. Some libraries have moved away from having a card catalog to a computer printout and/or terminal where all books, periodicals, and other matter in that particular library are listed.

3.26. Use 3-inch by 5-inch white lined cards to record your notes as you gather data for your paper. Hold the cards horizontally and write on the lines.

3.27. Do some preliminary research to be sure you can locate information and data easily on your chosen subject. Proceed as follows:

Develop a preliminary bibliography, placing one reference only on each of your cards. These references relate to the subject you will develop in your paper. One of the following general references may give you an overview of your subject as a basis for further development:

Academic American Encyclopedia

Collier's Encyclopedia

Encyclopedia Americana

The Encyclopaedia Britannica
Funk & Wagnalls New Encyclopedia
Harper World Encyclopedia
New American Encyclopedia
New Caxton Encyclopedia
New Columbia Encyclopedia
New Lincoln Library Encyclopedia
New Standard Dictionary
Pears Cyclopaedia
Random House Encyclopedia
University Desk Encyclopedia
Volume Library
The World Book Encyclopedia

3.28.   Other sources in the library that will help you locate information include the following tools:
card catalog, periodical indexes, rotary files, vertical files, or all three. See Nos. 3.31, 3.32–.34 for examples of the card catalog and periodical index. Vertical files are file cases in which are stored various and sundry matter such as booklets and catalogs received by the library. Consult the *Vertical File Index* for a listing of such material from 1935.

3.29.   The card catalog generally lists books and periodicals that are bound. Some libraries list audiovisual materials except films. The card catalog is made up of 3-inch by 5-inch unlined white cards either in type or print listing all books, reference books, and other contents of the library. See Nos. 3.31 and 3.32.

3.30.   The card catalog lists each book three ways:
author, title, and subject
See No. 3.31.

3.31.   The card catalog includes typed cards prepared by the local library.

---

* *A, An,* and *The* appearing as the first word in a title of a general reference are generally ignored in alphabetizing those references. The first letter of the next word determines the alphabetical order.

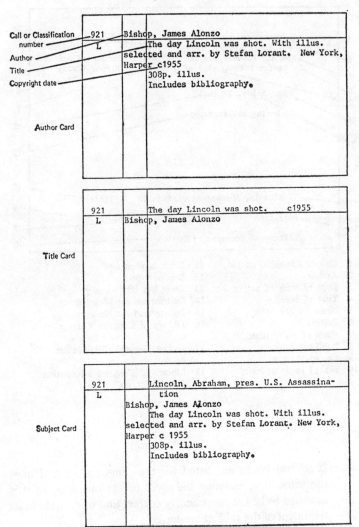

3.32. The card catalog also has printed cards obtained from the Library of Congress. These cards provide the same general information as the local library cards shown in No. 3.31.

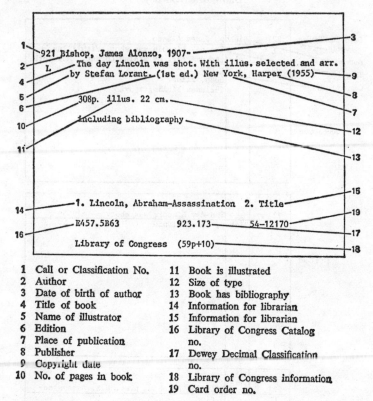

1 Call or Classification No.
2 Author
3 Date of birth of author
4 Title of book
5 Name of illustrator
6 Edition
7 Place of publication
8 Publisher
9 Copyright date
10 No. of pages in book

11 Book is illustrated
12 Size of type
13 Book has bibliography
14 Information for librarian
15 Information for librarian
16 Library of Congress Catalog
   no.
17 Dewey Decimal Classification
   no.
18 Library of Congress information
19 Card order no.

3.33.   If several books are listed for the same author and have the same title, examine the most recent one first, as it is assumed to be the most nearly correct and up-to-date in its treatment of the subject matter.

3.34.   If references are not listed under your subject title, you may be referred by "See" and "See also" cards to similar topics.

		Manslaughter	see
	Assassination Homicide Murder		

"See" Card

		Assassination	see also
	Anarchism and anarchists Murder Regicides Terrorism·		

"See also" Card

3.35. All books have author, subject, and title cards. For some
books, such as a collection of poems or biographies, another type of card may be prepared, known as an analytic
card. This card serves to call your attention to a small
portion of another book which carries information on
your subject.

For example, if you wished to write a term paper on the
assassination of Abraham Lincoln, you might note the
following reference on an analytic card if you were to
check the card catalog under Lincoln:

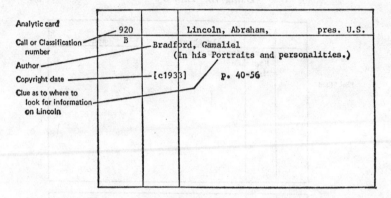

3.36. (a) The Dewey Decimal System classifies books numeri-
            cally:

000	General Works	500	Pure Science
100	Philosophy and Related Disciplines	600	Technology (Applied Science)
200	Religion	700	The Arts
300	The Social Sciences	800	Literature and Rhetoric
400	Language	900	General Geography and History

Note that the call or classification number of the book shown on
the analytic card above is 920. Also note that the Dewey Decimal
System reserves the 900 section for books on history.

(b) The Library of Congress System (often used in large
      university libraries) classifies books according to the
      alphabet:

A	General Works, Polygraphy, and Bibliography	H	Social Sciences
		J	Political Science
B	Philosophy, Psychology, and Religion	KF	Law of the United States
		L	Education
C	Auxiliary Sciences of History	M	Music and Books on Music
		N	Fine Arts
D	General and Old World History (except America)	P	Language and Literature
		Q	Science
E–F	American History	R	Medicine
G	Geography, Anthropology, Manners and Customs, Folklore, Recreation	S	Agriculture, Plant and Animal Industry, Fish Cul-

ture, and Fisheries,
Hunting Sports
T Technology
U Military Science

V Naval Science
Z Bibliography and Library Science

3.37. To ascertain whether any information on your topic is available in periodicals and newspapers, you would consult the many periodical and newspaper indexes available.

3.38. While periodical indexes may vary in style and arrangement, the following illustration shows the data usually given:

Readers' Guide to Periodical Literature.[1] General periodicals by author and subject from 1900.

Education in cooperation: new ventures reported. Lib J 100:1763 0 1 '75
  See also
Library institutes and workshops
1 ·LIBRARY science
        See also
  Cataloging.
  ·LIBRARY seminars. See Library institutes and workshops
  LIBRARY standards. See College libraries—Standards
  LIBRARY workshops. See Library institutes and workshops
  LIBYA
      Expropriation policy
  Blows at Hammer; Occidental petroleum's subsidiary. por Time 106:62 0 13 '75
      Politics and government
  Why Kaddafi piped down. B. Came. por Newsweek 86:36+ S 22 '75
  LICENSES
      See also
  Radio operators, Amateur—Licenses
2 LIDS, Canning jar. See Canning and preserving
      —Equipment and supplies
  LIE detectors and detection
  Right way to use a lie detector. D. T. Lykken. il por Psychol Today 8:56-60+ bibl (p98) Mr '75: Discussion. 9-12-13 Ag '75
3 Yes to lie detector tests for private employees; il Nations Bus 63:16 Ag '75

LIGHTNING
  See also
  Golf—Lightning hazards
LIGHTNING suppression (weather control) See Weather control
LIGHTS, Traffic. See Traffic signals
LILIES
  Lilies are for everyone. E. A. McRae. il Horticulture 53:26-8+ S '75   4
LIMBS, Artificial
  See also
  Hands, Artificial
LIMITATION OF ACTIONS
  Statutes of limitation: an overview. A. T.   5
    Kornblut. Archir Rec 158:49-50 Ag '75
LIN, C. C. and Van De Sande, J. H.   6
  Differential fluorescent staining of human chromosomes with daunomycin and adriamycin—the D-bands. bibl il Science 190: 7
    61-3 0 3 '75
LINCOLN, Abraham   8
      Addresses, messages, etc.—
  Reflections—the Gettysburg address. M. J.   9
    Adler and W. Gorman. New Yorker 51:42-
    4+ S 8 '75   10
      Asssasination
  True history of the assassination of Abraham Lincoln and the conspiracy of 1865. by L. 11
    Weichmann. Review—   12
      New Repub 173-91+2-S 20 '75. S. P.
    Lee—   13

1 "See" and "See also" references	8 Subheading
2 Article contains bibliography	9 Title of article
3 Article is illustrated	10 Article is continued in back of periodical
4 Volume number of periodical	11 Review of book
5 Date of periodical	12 Name of periodical
6 Page number of periodical	13 Author of article
7 Main heading	

3.39. *The Nineteenth Century Readers' Guide to Periodical Literature, 1890–99* includes author, subject, and illustrator

[1] *Readers' Guide to Periodical Literature* Copyright © 1975 by The H. W. Wilson Company. Material reproduced by permission of the publisher.

entries for short stories, novels, plays, and poems. Book reviews are also indexed.

3.40. Book indexes usually list most books published. These indexes are arranged by author, subject, and title. This index differs from the library card catalog which lists only books found in that particular library.

3.41. General periodical indexes are excellent starting points for locating information not generally found in books. The more common indexes are:

Christian Science Monitor Index, from 1960
Directory of Newspapers and Periodicals, from 1880
New York Times Index, from 1913
Poole's Index to Periodical Literature, 1802–1907
Readers' Guide to Periodical Literature, from 1900
Times Index, from 1906

3.42. *Guide to Reference Books* lists reference books basic to research. General and specific books and other printed matter are listed. It is extremely helpful in making a systematic study of reference books available, classified by subject matter.

3.43. In addition to the above, No. 3.42, you should consult *Introduction to Reference Work* by Katz (McGraw-Hill Book Company). Volume I provides basic information sources, and Volume II explains the various reference services available in the library.

3.44. Another important source for gathering information for your paper is to refer to specialized reference books. The following list, arranged by subject matter, should help you get started:

(a) Accounting, Banking, Business, Economics, Finance
Accountants Digest, from 1935. Subject index.
Applied Science and Technology Index, from 1958. Subject index.
Business Information: How to Find and Use It
Business Periodicals Index, from 1958. Accounting, advertising, automation, banking, finance, general business, insurance, labor and manage-

ment, taxation, transportation, specific busi-
nesses, industries, trade. Subject index.

Commercial Atlas and Marketing Guide

Dictionary of Data Processing

Dictionary of Economics

Encyclopedia of Accounting Systems

Encyclopedia of Banking and Finance

Encyclopedia of Management

*Encyclopedic Dictionary of Systems and Proce-
dures*

Financial Handbook

How to Use the Business Library

Industrial Arts Index, 1913–57. Changed to *Applied Science and Technology Index,* and *Business Periodicals Index* in 1958.

Insurance Periodical Index

Journal of Economic Literature

Predicast's F&S Index United States

Wall Street Journal Index, from 1957

(b) Agriculture, Biology, Chemistry, Medicine

Agriculture Engineer's Handbook, from 1961

Applied Science and Technology Index, from
1958. Geology, metallurgy, physics. Subject index. Formerly, *Industrial Arts Index.*

Bibliography of the History of Medicine

Biological Abstracts, from 1926

Biological and Agricultural Index, from 1964.
Agriculture, biology, forestry, home economics,
veterinary medicine. Subject index. Until 1964,
listed as *Agricultural Index.*

Biology Data Book

Biology and Medicine

Blakiston's New Gould Medical Dictionary

Chemical Abstracts, from 1907

Cumulated Index Medicus, from 1960. Author and
subject index.

Current List of Medical Literature, from 1941

Drug Interaction: An Annotated Bibliography
with Selected Excerpts, 1967–70

Encyclopedia of Chemistry

Encyclopedia of Food
Environmental Abstracts, 1971–73
Grzimek's Animal Life Encyclopedia
Handbook of Biochemistry and Molecular Biology
Handbook of Chemistry and Physics
Index Medicus, 1879–1927. Author and subject index.
Taber's Cyclopedic Medical Dictionary

(c)   Anthropology

Abstracts in Anthropology
Abstracts of Folklore Studies
American Negro Reference Book
Dictionary of Anthropology
Harvard Encyclopedia of American Ethnic Groups
International Bibliography of Social and Cultural Anthropology
The Negro Almanac
Peoples of All Nations
A Study in Race & Culture Contacts
When Peoples Meet

(d)   Art, Music

Art Index, from 1929. Archaeology, architecture, arts and crafts, ceramics, decoration and ornament graphic arts, industrial design, interior decoration, landscape architecture, painting, sculpture. Author and subject index.
Catalog of Museum Publications and Media, from 1980
Complete Opera Book
Dictionary of Modern Sculpture
Dictionary of Musical Terms
Encyclopedia of the Arts
Encyclopedia of World Art
Guide to Art Reference Books
Guide to the Performing Arts, from 1957
Harvard Dictionary of Music
Music Index, from 1949. Author and subject index.
New Grove Dictionary of Music and Musicians

The New Kobbé's Complete Opera Book
The Oxford Companion to Art
A Standard History of Music

(e) Biography

American Men and Women of Science
Appleton's Cyclopedia of American Biography
Biography Index, from 1947. Indexed by profession and occupation.
Chambers's Biographical Dictionary
Contemporary Authors
Current Biography Yearbook, from 1940
Dictionary of American Biography, 1928–37. Important people in American history no longer living.
Dictionary of American Scholars; a biographical directory
Dictionary of International Biography
Dictionary of National Biography, 1882–1967. Important people in English history.
The International Who's Who
Leaders in Education
McGraw-Hill Encyclopedia of World Biography
Webster's American Biographies
Webster's Biographical Dictionary
Who Was Who in America
Who's Who, from 1948. Important living English persons.
Who's Who in America, from 1899
Who's Who in American Education
Who's Who in the East
The Writer's Directory

(f) Education

American Library Directory
Bibliographic Guide to Educational Research
Business Education Index
Canadian Education Index
Current Index to Journals in Education (CIJE)
Dictionary of Education
Dissertation Abstracts International
Education Abstracts, 1949–65

Educational Administration Abstracts
Education Index, from 1929. Child study, comparative education, curriculum development, educational psychology, educational research, elementary education, higher education, school administration, secondary education, statistical methods, teacher education, and related subjects. Subject index.
Educational Resources Information Center (ERIC)
Encyclopedia of Education
Encyclopedia of Educational Research
How to Locate Educational Information and Data
Research in Education (ERIC), from 1966
Resources in Education/ERIC
Review of Educational Research
Statistical Yearbook, from 1963
Thesaurus of ERIC Descriptors

(g) Energy and the Environment
The Energy Index
The Environmental Index
International Aerospace Abstracts
Nuclear Science Abstracts
Oceanic Abstracts, from 1978
Pollution Abstracts, from 1971

(h) Engineering, Science, Technology
Abstracts & Indexes in Science & Technology: A Descriptive Guide
Aerospace Yearbook
American Men and Women of Science
Applied Science and Technology Index, from 1958. Aeronautics, automation, chemistry, construction, electricity, electrical communication, engineering, geology, metallurgy, industrial and related subjects. Replaces the *Industrial Arts Index.*
Engineer's Year-Book, from 1894
A Guide to Information in Space Science and Technology
Industrial Arts Index, 1913–57. Engineering, trade, business. Ceased publication in 1957; re-

placed by *Applied Science and Technology Index* and the *Business Periodicals Index*. Subject index.

International Aerospace Abstracts, from 1961

McGraw-Hill Encyclopedia of Science and Technology

Nuclear Science Abstracts, from 1948

Sources of Engineering Information

Van Nostrand's Scientific Encyclopedia

(i)   Geology, Geography

Aids to Geographical Research

Annotated Bibliography of Economic Geology

Bibliography and Index of Geology Exclusive of North America, from 1934. Subject index.

Bibliography of North American Geology

Encyclopedia of World Regional Geology, from 1975

Geological Abstracts

Geological Dictionary

Guide to Geologic Literature

Social Sciences and Humanities Index, from 1916. Formerly *International Index*. Author and subject index.

Webster's New Geographical Dictionary

(j)   History

America: History and Life

American Historical Documents

The Beards' New Basic History of the United States

Current Digest of the Soviet Press

Dictionary of American History

Dictionary of Dates

Encyclopedia of American History

An Encyclopedia of World History

Guide to Historical Literature

Guide to Historical Reading

Harvard Guide to American History

Historical Abstracts

Historical Atlas

Webster's Guide to American History

(k) Language, Acronyms, Synonyms, Proverbs, Quotations

Acronyms, Initialisms, and Abbreviations Dictionary

Allen's Synonyms and Antonyms

Dictionary of Acronyms and Abbreviations

Dictionary of American Proverbs and Proverbial Phrases, 1820–80

Dictionary of American Slang

Dictionary of Contemporary American Usage

Early American Proverbs & Proverbial Phrases

Familiar Quotations by Bartlett

FPA Book of Quotations

The Home Book of Bible Quotations

Hoyt's New Cyclopedia of Practical Quotations

Language and Language Behavioral Abstracts

The Modern Dictionary of Quotations

Oxford Dictionary of Quotations

The Quotation Dictionary

Quotations for All Occasions

Quotations for Speakers

Racial Proverbs

Roget's International Thesaurus

Roget's Thesaurus of Synonyms and Antonyms

Speech Index, 1935–61. Author, subject and type of speech index.

Standard Handbook of Synonyms, Antonyms, and Prepositions

Stevenson's Home Book of Quotations

Webster's New Dictionary of Synonyms

(l) Literature

Articles on American Literature, 1900–1950

Book Review Digest, from 1905

Book Review Index

Cambridge History of American Literature

Cassell's Encyclopedia of World Literature

Contemporary Literary Criticism

Essay and General Literature Index

A Glossary of Literary Terms

Granger's Index to Poetry
Guide to American Literature and Its Background,
    since 1890
McGraw-Hill Encyclopedia of World Drama
The Oxford Companion to American Literature
Play Index
The Reader's Companion to World Literature
The Reader's Encyclopedia
Short Story Index

(m) Mathematics, Physics

CRC Handbook of Mathematical Sciences
Encyclopedia of Computer Sciences and Technology
Encyclopedic Dictionary of Mathematics
Guide to the Literature of Mathematics and Physics
Handbook of Chemistry and Physics
Mathematics Dictionary
Physics Abstracts
World of Mathematics

(n) Folklore, Mythology

A Bibliography of North American Folklore and Folksong
Abstracts of Folklore Studies
Folklore Index
Folklore of the American Negro Mythologies
Folksong Style & Culture
Mythology of All Races
Religions, Mythologies, Folklore
Religions of the World
Treasury of American Folklore
A Treasury of American Superstitions

(o) Nations, Political Science

A Guide to the Use of United States Documents
Handbook of Latin American Studies
Index to Latin American Periodical Literature,
    1929–60. Economics, politics, government.
    Author and subject index.
International Bibliography of Political Science

International Political Science Abstracts
Public Affairs Information Service Bulletin (PAIS), from 1915
Worldmark Encyclopedia of the Nations

(p) Philosophy

Bibliography of Philosophical Bibliographies
Dictionary of Philosophy and Psychology
Encyclopedia of Philosophy
Handbook in the History of Philosophy

(q) Psychology

American Men and Women of Science
Dictionary of Behavioral Science
Dictionary of Philosophy and Psychology
Dictionary of Psychology
Encyclopedia of Psychology
Encyclopedia of Sexual Behavior
Harvard List of Books in Psychology
Psychological Abstracts, from 1927
Psychological Index, 1895–1931. Author index.
Thesaurus of Psychological Index Terms

(r) Radio, Television

Educational Media Index, 1964. Master title index.
Encyclopedic Dictionary of Electronics and Nuclear Engineering
Guides to Newer Educational Media
International Television Almanac, from 1956
Radio Amateur's Handbook
Radio-Television-Electronic Dictionary
Sources of Information on Educational Media
Television Almanac
Television Manual
What's the Right Word?

(s) Recreation, Sports

Bibliography of Swimming
The Dictionary of Sports
Early American Sports
Encyclopedia of Sports
How-to-Do-it Book

Hunter's Encyclopedia

Index to Handicrafts, Model-making, and Workshop Projects. Subject index.

Official Encyclopedia of Baseball

Traditional Games of England, Scotland, and Ireland

(t)   Religion

The American Book of Days

Catholic Periodical and Literature Index, from 1930

Dictionary of the Bible

Encyclopedia Judaica

Encyclopedia of Religion and Ethics

A Guide to American Catholic History

The Home Book of Bible Quotations

Index to Jewish Periodicals, from 1963. Selected American and Anglo-Jewish journals. Author and subject index.

Index to Religious Periodical Literature, from 1960. Basically Protestant with some Jewish and Roman Catholic listings. Author and subject index.

Jewish Encyclopedia

New Catholic Encyclopedia

Religions, Mythologies, Folklore

(u)   Social Science

Abstracts for Social Workers

Abstracts on Criminology and Penology

British Humanities Index

Crime and Delinquency Abstracts

Criminology Index (1945–72)

Current Contents: Social and Behavioral Sciences

Demographic Yearbook

Dissertational Abstracts International

Encyclopedia of Social Work

Encyclopedia of the Social Sciences

A Guide to Periodical Literature in the Social Sciences and the Humanities, 1955–65. Renamed *Social Sciences Citation Index,* from 1973

Humanities Index, from 1974. Supersedes in part *Social Sciences and Humanities Index.* Archaeology, classics, folklore, history, language, literature, performing arts, philosophy, religion, and related subjects. Author and subject index.

Human Resources Index

International Encyclopedia of the Social Sciences

International Index, 1907–52. Renamed *Social Sciences Index,* 1953–64. Renamed *Social Sciences and Humanities Index,* from 1966. Author and subject index.

Psychological Abstracts

Public Affairs Information Service Bulletin (PAIS), from 1915

Readers' Guide to Periodical Literature

Social Sciences and Humanities Index

Social Sciences Citation Index

Sources of Information in the Social Sciences

Women's Studies Abstracts

(v) United States, Public Documents

The Book of the States, from 1935

Dictionary of American History, 1940–44

Documents of American History, 1962

Monthly Catalog of United States Government Publications, from 1895

Official Congressional Record

A Popular Guide to Government Publications, 1951–62. Subject index.

Public Affairs Information Service Bulletin (PAIS)

Readex Microprint, from 1953. Author and subject index.

Statistical Abstract of the United States, from 1878

3.45. Almanac, and general yearbooks, provide valuable information for developing a paper. Some of the more important ones are listed below:

Almanack, from 1869 (British)

Americana Annual, from 1923
American Yearbook, from 1910
Collier's Encyclopedia Year Book, from 1939
Demographic Yearbook, from 1948
Economic Almanac, from 1940
Facts on File, Weekly News Digest with Cumulative Index, from 1940
Guinness Book of World Records, from 1964
Information Please Almanac, from 1947
Public Affairs Information Service Bulletin (PAIS), from 1915
Reader's Digest Almanac
Statesman's Year-book, from 1864
Statistical Abstract of the United States, from 1878
World Almanac and Book of Facts, from 1868
World Book Year Book, from 1962
Yearbook of Agriculture, from 1894
Yearbook of the United Nations, from 1946

3.46.   Atlases contain maps and economic information. Some of the most recent include:
Encyclopaedia Britannica World Atlas
Goode's World Atlas
Oxford World Atlas
Rand McNally Commercial Atlas and Marketing Guide
Rand McNally New Cosmopolitan World Atlas
Rand McNally Premier World Atlas

3.47.   Word dictionaries are essential for developing a paper. The following dictionaries are up to date and extremely helpful:
The American Heritage Dictionary
Funk & Wagnall's New Standard Dictionary
The Oxford English Dictionary
Random House Dictionary of the English Language
Thorndike Barnhardt Dictionary
Webster's New Collegiate Dictionary
Webster's New International Dictionary
Webster's Third New International Dictionary

Italian, French, German, Russian, and Spanish dictionaries are also in print.

3.48. Microforms have added tremendously to the storehouse of knowledge contained in the library and offer great promise for providing information for your paper. You will need the librarian's help to locate:

Guide to Microforms in Print
Newspapers on Microfilm
Readex Microprint
Subject Guide to Microforms in Print
Union List of Microforms
A Union List of Publications in Opaque Microforms

3.49. To determine if a particular book is in print, consult:

Book Review Digest, from 1905. "See" and "See also" references included.

Books in Print, from 1948. Author and subject index.

Cumulative Book Index, from 1929. Monthly supplements to the *United States Catalogue.* Includes all books published in the United States except textbooks and also includes books published and printed in the English language anywhere in the world. Listed by author, subject, and title. Useful in reading about a subject when the book is not found in the local library.

Paperbound Books in Print, from 1955. Author and subject index.

United States Catalog: Books in Print

United States Catalogue, from 1928. Books published in the United States on a particular subject.

3.50. Many libraries have special facilities for disabled library users and their aids. Resources in special formats (large type, Braille), specialized equipment (magnifying glasses, talking book players, electric page turner, lap stand, etc.) and special services available by telephone may be present in the library you frequent. Inquire of the Coordinator of Library Services for the Disabled or of some librarian of the facilities available, if you require special assistance.

CHAPTER 4

PREPARING THE BIBLIOGRAPHY

Do not become overwhelmed by the abundance of material that may be available on your subject. Select your bibliography with care, so that it is not cluttered with references of little, if any, value to you. Spend considerable time on this bibliography because it will pay you dividends, not only in the opportunity it provides you to broaden your understanding and knowledge of your subject but also in the clues and ideas it offers which will help you develop your paper.

4.1. A working bibliography is a list of the sources of information selected by you.

4.2. The final bibliography appears at the end of the term paper and lists only those references that you use from your working bibliography.

4.3. Each reference in your working bibliography is recorded in ink on separate 3 by 5 cards.

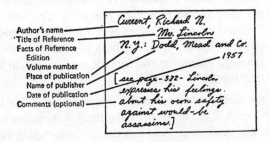

Author's name
Title of Reference
Facts of Reference
Edition
Volume number
Place of publication
Name of publisher
Date of publication
Comments (optional)

Current, Richard N.
Mr. Lincoln
N.Y.: Dodd, Mead and Co.
1957
[see page - 382 - Lincoln expresses his feelings about his own safety against would-be assassins.]

4.4. A typical term paper usually requires as many as 50 bibliographic references even though all are not included in the writing of the paper.

4.5. As you prepare your working bibliography, you will constantly be adding new cards and eliminating others.

4.6. By pruning, screening, adding, and deleting cards, your working bibliography develops into your final bibliography, which is a selected list of references far fewer in number than you originally had.

4.7. Examine appropriate books for information on your subject, quickly checking the table of contents, chapter headings, and index. Check for a bibliography at ends of chapters and at the end of the book.

4.8. After completing your first bibliography, prune or screen it by removing and placing in a separate pack the references that hold little promise of information about your subject. Save all cards in case you need the references later.

4.9. If a book reference holds promise, go to the card catalog and write the classification number in the upper left-hand corner of your 5 by 3 card.
See Nos. 3.31–.32.

4.10. If a periodical reference holds promise for you, check with your librarian to see if the library carries that particular magazine or newspaper.

NOTE: In the bibliographic and footnote listings throughout the text of this book *italic type* is used for those items that should be underlined in your paper, since you are not expected to reproduce this type. You will see also that certain abbreviations and foreign expressions customarily appear in *italics,* both in this book and in your reading. Whenever you include such words in a paper, they should be underlined.

4.11. If the bibliographic citation is more than one line long, indent each line (other than the first) five spaces from the left margin. Notice how this differs from typing footnotes. Compare footnotes on Term Paper Page 3 with Bibliography.

4.12. A proper form for listing references both for the working bibliographic cards and for the final bibliography for the term paper is illustrated below. The bibliography appears in alphabetical order with family name first at the end of the term paper. For each bibliography sample shown, the way it appears as a footnote is explained in Chapter 8. Italicized words, when typed, are underscored, as are the spaces between the words.

See 8.25 a–z.

Book

a. Anonymous works

> *Textbooks Are Indispensable!* New York: The American Textbook Publishers Institute [n.d.].

b. One author

> Buckley, William F. Jr. *Atlantic High.* Garden City, NY: Doubleday & Company, Inc., 1982.

c. Two or three authors

> Greenberg, S. F. and Valletutti, Paul J. *Stress and the Helping Professions.* Baltimore: Paul H. Brookes, 1980.

d. More than three authors

> Aberbach, Joel, and others. *Bureaucrats and Politicians in Western Democracies.* Boston: Harvard University Press, 1981.

e. Editor as author

> Peck, William T., ed. *Washington's Farewell Address and Webster's Bunker Hill Orations.* New York: The Macmillan Company, 1909.

f. Edited by a person other than the author

> Colburn, William, and Weinberg, Sanford. *An Orientation to Listening and Audience Analysis.* Edited by Ronald Applebaum and Roderick Hart. Chicago: Science Research Associates, 1980.

g. Edition other than the first

> Taber, Clarence Wilbur. *Taber's Cyclopedia Medical Dictionary.* 14th ed. Philadelphia: F. A. Davis Company, 1981.

h. Review

> Schedler, N. Review of *Environmental Ethics,* by K. A. Shrader-Prechette. *Defenders,* August 1982, pp. 33–34.

i.   Citing work in more than one volume
     Hoy, Cyrus. *Introductions, Notes, and Commentaries to
     Texts in the Dramatic Works of Thomas Dekker.* Vol. 1.
     New York: Cambridge University Press, 1980.

Encyclopedia article

j.   Author listed
     McGraw-Hill Encyclopedia of Science and Technology,
     1977 ed., Vol. 12, s.v. "Sensory Learning," by Kao L.
     Chow.
k.   No author listed
     Encyclopedia Americana, 1980 ed. S.v. "Navajo Moun-
     tain."

Government document

l.   Author listed
     Blehar, Mary C. "Families and Public Policy." *National
     Institute on Mental Health Monographs.* Washington,
     DC: U.S. Department of Health, Education, and Wel-
     fare, 1979.
m.   No author listed
     U.S. Department of Commerce, Bureau of the Census.
     Statistical Abstract of the United States. Washington,
     DC: Government Printing Office, 1979.

Newspaper article

n.   Author listed
     Montgomery, Paul L. "Garden Plot Is at Center of West
     Side Fight," *New York Times,* 9 August 1982, Sec. A,
     p. 1.
o.   No author listed
     "Unemployment Soars to Record 9.8 Percent," *Mobile
     (AL) Press-Register,* 7 August 1982.
p.   Editorial
     "Confusion over Taiwan." Editorial. *Albany* (NY)
     Times Union, 23 August 1982, p. 7.

Periodical or magazine article

q. Author listed

Findley, Rowe. "Our National Forests: Problems in Paradise." *National Geographic,* 162, September 1982, pp. 306–25; 332–39.

r. No author listed

"ERA Dies." *Time,* 5 July 1982, pp. 28–32.

Miscellaneous

s. Collected works

Cohen, Morton N., ed. *The Selected Letters of Lewis Carroll.* New York: Pantheon Books, 1982.

t. Interview

James, Fob, Governor of Alabama, Interview at the Executive Mansion, Montgomery, 1 July 1982.

u. Letter

Letter by George A. Custer on file in the National Archives, Washington, DC [n.d.].

v. Pamphlet or Bulletin in a series

United Cerebral Palsy Association. *What Everyone Should Know About Cerebral Palsy.* New York: UCP Inc., 1977.

w. Quarterly

Burns, Arthur F. "U.S. Relations with West Germany." *The Atlantic Community Quarterly,* 20 (Summer 1982): 153–57.

x. Unpublished doctoral dissertation

Roberts, Anne F. "Library Instruction for Librarians." D.A. Dissertation, State University of New York at Albany, 1982.

y. Translation

Yalouris, Nicholas. *Alexander the Great and His Heritage.* Translated by David Hardy. Boston: New York Graphic Society, 1980.

z. Yearbook article

Watson, Marjorie. "Mainstreaming the Educable Mentally Retarded." *Yearbook of Special Education, 1978–79.* Chicago: Marquis Who's Who, Inc., 1978.

CHAPTER 5

TAKING NOTES

Once you have developed an adequate bibliography, you are ready to take notes. Here is the heart of your research, so do not hurry it. Be sure to write plainly in order to avoid transcription errors later, and include a source reference on each card to simplify your footnoting job (*see Chapter 8*). Remember that the accuracy of the facts in your paper depends on the accuracy of your notes.

5.1. In the process of using your working bibliography, you make note of any information of value to your term paper.

5.2. Develop an orderly, systematic, and scholarly routine for notetaking.

It is important that you include all pertinent information such as complete reference to the source. Before you leave the source, double-check the reference and content for accuracy. This will save time looking it up later.

5.3. You will take more notes than you need to complete your paper. It is better to have too much information, which can be pruned for basic essentials, than to have so little that you must search for more at the last minute.

5.4. Be critical of what you read, and write sparingly, keeping your notes to a minimum.

5.5. The use of white lined cards for notetaking makes it easy to sort, eliminate, and arrange data into logical sequence. It is not always possible to tell what is relevant as you take notes.

Even though some of your notes may seem to have little

value, do not dispose of them. Put them in a separate pack and label HOLD just in case you need them later.

5.6. Use a larger size card for notetaking to avoid mix-up with the smaller bibliographic cards.

5.7. Carry spare cards with you at all times, as evidence sometimes presents itself in strange places.

5.8. Avoid unusual abbreviations as a form of shorthand in notetaking, for you run the risk of failing to transcribe accurately, particularly when a quotation is involved.

5.9. Write on one side of the card. If you must continue onto a second card, write "continued" at the top and number each card such as 1A, 1B.

5.10. Place only one idea on each card.
    See No. 5.11.

5.11. Notes may be of the following types: quotation, paraphrase, personal comment.
    See No. 5.17.

5.12. At the top center of each card, on the red line, write the type of note you are making.
    See Nos. 5.11 to 5.17.

5.13. Each card should have a descriptive label consisting of a main heading and subheading.
    See Nos. 5.11 to 5.17.

5.14. Each card contains three essential items of information:
    Reference to the source
    Descriptive label
    Body
    See Nos. 5.11 to 5.17.

5.15. Read the reference thoroughly before writing your note and then digest what you have read into one key idea.

5.16. Notes which summarize, comment upon the text, and/or evaluate what you have read are superior to quotation notes because more of YOU is put into the paper and that is what your instructor desires.

5.17. Recording essential information when you are reading a reference for the purpose of taking notes will save you

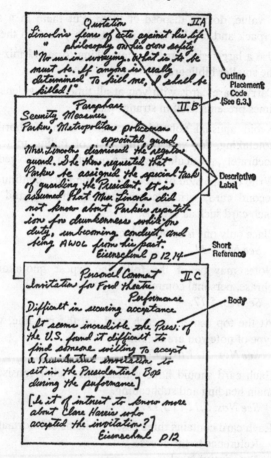

Outline
Placement
Code
(See 6.3.)

Descriptive
Label

Short
Reference

Body

time later. Then you will not have to go back in the final stages of your work when you are writing or typing the paper to obtain facts which are so easily obtainable during notetaking.

Identify sources of information in the short form (see No. above paraphrase card) by including the author's last name unless your bibliography lists more than one book by the same name, or more than one person with the same name.

5.18. Identify facts and opinions in your notes.

If the author expresses a personal opinion, record it as such in your notes and preface his opinion with the phrase, "according to the author," or some similar phrase.

5.19. Facts of common knowledge need not be documented.

Such statements as "John Wilkes Booth killed the President" and "Abraham Lincoln was President during the American Civil War" are common knowledge and need not be documented or carry a footnote reference.

5.20. Statements (a) which have questionable validity and/or (b) are controversial in nature, and/or (c) which contain little-known facts must be documented.

a. Statements open to question should be documented. For example, if you were to use the statement, "Alcohol consumption during pregnancy causes birth defects," it would be necessary and important to know who said it, since the medical profession is divided on the subject.

b. A controversial statement, such as "Smoking causes stunted growth," needs to be documented.

c. A little-known fact, such as "Contrary to popular belief, the Indians who massacred General Custer and his 7th Cavalry were armed for the most part with bows and arrows while only a few Indians were equipped with repeater rifles," should be documented.

5.21. Laws and formulas should appear as quotations.

5.22. Copy quotations exactly including punctuation, spelling, capitalization, paragraphing, and errors.

5.23. Use quotations only when you wish to retain the exact wording of the author because his statement is not clear, is of great significance, or is of a challenging nature.

5.24. Ellipses are used to indicate the omission of a few words from a quotation when such omissions are irrelevant to your subject. *See Term Paper Page 8.*

     a. Use three spaced dots when the omission is at the beginning or in the middle of a sentence.

     b. Use three spaced dots plus a period (four spaced dots) when the omission occurs at the end of a sentence.

     See Term Paper Page 8.

5.25. When ellipses end a quotation, place the ellipses inside the quotation mark.

5.26. Indicate the omission of an entire paragraph or more by a full line of doubled spaced periods (ellipses).
     See Term Paper Page 8, 11.

5.27. When you wish to insert your own words within a quotation, place brackets [ ] around your words.
     See Term Paper Page 3.

5.28. If you note an error in your reference and you wish to call this error to the attention of your reader, copy the quotation exactly as it appears in the original, follow the error with the word *sic* placed in brackets, and then make the correction.

5.29. Keep your completed notes on file until your term paper has been returned by your instructor.

CHAPTER 6

MAKING THE OUTLINE

After you have prepared your note cards, you are ready to make your first outline. It may be necessary to revise this outline several times. Work it out with great care, for you are only one step away from writing the first draft of your paper.

6.1. An outline enumerates important ideas to be developed in the paper.

6.2. An outline keeps you from wandering by forcing you to clarify your thinking about your subject.

As your outline begins to develop, gaps in your research (note card information) will be apparent and you will then see where additional research is needed.

6.3. There is a relationship between the outline and the note cards.

The usual procedure is to base the outline on the note cards. It is better to prepare the outline after the notes have been completed, even though it *is* possible to prepare the outline before taking your notes. Refer to the three note cards in No. 5.17. The outline placement code appearing in the upper right-hand corner of each card was placed there as a result of having arranged the note cards in some order. The quotation card was assigned the code IIA, the paraphrase card was given the outline code IIB, and the personal comment card was assigned IIC.

See No. 5.17 and the topic and sentence outline in No. 6.13.

6.4. If you prepare your outline from your notes, you may want to spread your note cards on the floor and put them back together again in logical order.

6.5. An outline should provide a guide for writing a term paper. It may list items in their order of time occurrence.

If the term paper is on Lincoln's assassination, your *first* outline might appear as follows:

LINCOLN'S ASSASSINATION
I. Before the assassination
II. The assassination
III. After the assassination

6.6. An outline may also develop by expanding the main thought without regard to chronological arrangement.

LINCOLN'S ASSASSINATION—AN UNSOLVED MYSTERY
I. The act itself
II. Grant's strange behavior
III. Mrs. Lincoln's unfortunate choice of bodyguard
IV. The President's premonition
V. Booth's strange revelations

6.7. Your outline can change to suit your purpose. You are not shackled to the first one you prepare. Constant revision of your outline will develop it to full maturity.

Note how the outlines on Lincoln's assassination in Nos. 6.5, 6.6, 6.11, and the topic and sentence outline in 6.13 change as they mature.

6.8. The outline must indicate a reason for your paper. It must show relationships between facts, and it must come to a logical conclusion.

Avoid words like Introduction, Body, and Summary in your outline. They are vague and do not contribute to the development of your paper. Specific headings are needed.

6.9. Avoid too many main headings but have at least three.

The following outline form illustrates too fine a breakdown:

I.
  A.
    1.
    2.
      a.
      b.
        (1)
        (2)
          (a)
          (b)
            ((1))
            ((2))
  B.

6.10. If you list a I, you must also have a II. This is true for all subdivisions.

6.11. All main headings such as I, II, and III should be of the same value.

Unequal headings	*Equal headings*
LINCOLN'S ASSASSINATION	LINCOLN'S ASSASSINATION
I. Events leading to the murder	I. Events leading to the murder
II. The murder	II. The murder
III. Confusing news reports	III. Booth's escape
IV. Sgt. Cobb	IV. Booth's accomplices
V. Patrolman Parker	

6.12. Have all periods in main heading numbers line up. This also applies to all subdivisions.

6.13. Although a topic outline is easier to prepare, a sentence outline is preferred because it makes the writer really think about his or her subject and will result in an easier task and a superior paper.

    Notice in the following partial outlines how the sentence outline brings the student closer to the point of writing his or her paper.

TOPIC OUTLINE

Lincoln's Assassination—A Murder Mystery

I. Purpose of the paper
II. Lincoln—before the assassination
   A. His premonition of approaching death
     1. Dreams
     2. Philosophy
     3. Conversations
   B. His lack of security protection
     1. Unreliable personal bodyguard
     2. Lock on theater presidential box broken
     3. Peephole bored through box door undetected
   C. His difficulty in obtaining guests for the performance
     1. Grant to be honored with Lincoln at theater
     2. Grant accepts President's invitation
     3. Grant declines invitation
     4. Lincoln finds himself without guests
III. The assassination
   A. A look at the assassin
   B. Motives for murder
   C. The shooting
   D. Stanton's famous last words
IV. After the assassination
   A. Booth's escape into Maryland
     1. Passed through guard post
     2. Received medical aid from physician
     3. Hidden by southern sympathizers
   B. Stanton's lack of co-operation
     1. Refused to give Booth's name to press
     2. Disinterested in capture of John Surrat
   C. The accomplices
   D. The trial

The final outline appears in sentence form. Every heading and subdivision is a complete statement.

SENTENCE OUTLINE*

LINCOLN'S ASSASSINATION—A MURDER MYSTERY

I. The purpose of this paper is to identify unexplained events in connection with the death of Abraham Lincoln.

    A. Records of the assassination reveal gaps and inconsistencies of the events leading up to and following the murder.

    B. John Wilkes Booth killed Lincoln, but why he did it and the full details of his diabolical plan leave many questions unanswered.

II. Lincoln had been marked for death by several people during his term in office, but efforts to protect his life went unnoticed.

    A. Before his death, Lincoln had suspected that he would be killed at the hands of an assassin.

        1. He was extremely melancholy on the day of the shooting, having been troubled by bad dreams.

        2. His philosophy on his own safety reflected a fatalistic attitude.

        3. He said "good-bye" rather than "good night" as he left the White House for the theater.

    B. The President was not provided with adequate security measures.

        1. The regular guard was dismissed and a discredited police officer was assigned to guard his life.

            a. Patrolman Parker had been officially reprimanded for drunkenness on several occasions.

            b. Parker had been found guilty of conduct unbecoming an officer on several occasions.

* See Term Paper pages 1, 2, 3 and note how this sentence outline develops into paragraphs to become a term paper.

     c. Parker had been known to leave his post without proper leave on several occasions.

  2. The lock on the door leading to the presidential box was broken.

  3. A peephole that had been bored in the door leading to the presidential box went unnoticed.

6.14. If asked, submit your outline to your instructor for his or her approval. You may save yourself time and heartache.

CHAPTER 7

WRITING THE PAPER

Very few people are naturally gifted writers. For most of us, writing is a difficult task. To do a creditable job it will be necessary for you to rework paragraphs and labor over some of your sentences as you try to find the word that expresses the precise thought you have in mind. Above all, do not get discouraged now. Other students are going through the same experience and those who persevere and rise above their discouragements will finally achieve their goal, a term paper of which they can be proud.

7.1. Do not delay writing until the last possible moment. You cannot do a good job if you rush it. Allow yourself ample time.

7.2. Keep within the number of words set for your paper by your instructor.
A minimum of 2,000 words is usually required.

7.3. Choose a final title that is interesting, clear, and brief.
See Term Paper Title Page.

7.4. Your instructor will probably be influenced by your opening and closing paragraphs, so make them especially good.

7.5. Not even the most experienced writer can hope that his or her first draft will be the best draft.
Prepare yourself to write several drafts before your paper is in its final form.

7.6. During your first draft, start writing and do not be concerned with grammar or sentence construction. You can correct this later. The important thing is to *get started*.

7.7. Avoid merely copying your notes. This makes the reading dull, choppy, and lacks the most essential element, YOU.

7.8. Avoid colloquialisms and slang expressions.

7.9. If you have a choice between using a simple word or a technical one, choose the simpler word your reader will understand.

His remuneration for the week was in excess of $200.
His pay for the week was more than $200.

7.10. Try to avoid making any personal references to yourself such as *I, me, mine,* or *the writer.* Keep personal pronouns out of the paper if possible.

7.11. Have a dictionary and a thesaurus handy and consult them.

7.12. Write the first draft with your notes and outline before you. Use the outline as your writing guide and your notes to recall the facts. Do not write your paper by copying your notes.

7.13. Use wide margins and triple space your first draft to allow room for corrections.

7.14. Use separate sheets of paper for each paragraph in your draft. This will allow you to add to your paragraphs during your revision and to insert footnotes without fear of crowding your work.

7.15. Write or type on one side of 8½- by 11-inch paper which is of quality good enough to take erasing and editing.

7.16. Prepare a carbon copy in case your instructor wishes to see your draft. Term papers *have* been lost.

7.17. If asked, submit a clean copy of your revised draft to your instructor. Type it if possible.

7.18. Allow one-half inch (three lines) for each footnote.

7.19. Documenting and footnoting are closely related. To document means to cite quotations in the text; to footnote means to list the exact reference of the quotation.
See Term Paper Page 8.

7.20. Document and footnote as you write your draft. You might forget one or the other if you hold off doing this until your final copy is being prepared. (*See Chapter 8* for the form and content of footnotes.)

7.21. When using a quotation, work it into the text smoothly with a transitional sentence.
See Term Paper Page 9.

7.22. Quoted matter should not take up more than one fifth of your paper. The remainder of your text comes from your own ideas.

7.23. Long quotations do not have quotation marks, are single spaced and indented five spaces from the left and right margins of the context.
See Term Paper Page 11.

7.24. Rather than copy a quotation, staple or clip the quotation note card to your draft. This saves time and ensures against an error during the copying.

7.25. Avoid using quoted matter unless it is absolutely essential that the words of another be included.

7.26. Acknowledge all paraphrases by using a superscript after the material and then listing it in the footnotes. Don't pass someone else's ideas off as your own.
See Term Paper Page 6.

7.27. Determine whether the paragraphs of your first draft are in logical order. If not, change them.

7.28. Every paragraph should have a key, or topic sentence—usually at its beginning.
See Term Paper Page 6.

7.29. Have medium and short paragraphs for interest.

7.30. If you include a summary paragraph, it should be short and concise and should answer the question in your opening paragraph, if that is the way your paper begins.
See Term Paper Page 8.

7.31. After your first writing, lay the paper aside for at *least a day*. Then when your outlook is fresh, pick it up and criticize it ruthlessly. It is far better for you to do this than to have the criticisms come from your instructor.

See No. 7.34.

7.32. Internally examine the paper for unity, coherence, and structure. Ask yourself:

Does the central theme hold together well?

Does the paper express itself clearly?

Is the paper well put together grammatically?

Other questions which will help you evaluate your paper can be found in the term paper checklist following the sample term paper on pages 117 and 118.

7.33. It may be necessary for you to clip and paste your first draft in different order for a more logical arrangement.

From your pasted draft, prepare your final copy.

7.34. Review and edit the final draft before typing the copy which you will submit to your instructor. This means that you may need to correct grammar, switch paragraphs, change words, delete irrelevant material, sharpen sentences to pinpoint thoughts, and add appropriate tables.

7.35. Check all footnotes and bibliographic entries for consistency of form and to see that all essential information is included.

7.36. Through constant pruning of irrelevant material, you may find your final copy shorter than your draft.

7.37. If the final copy sounds like a learned academician rather than like you, this difference will also be noted by your instructor. Now is the time to make changes that will reflect your own personality rather than to submit a paper that sounds like someone who possesses a number of college degrees.

7.38. The finished paper should include a title page, table of contents (optional), text, and a bibliography, in that order.

See Term Paper.

7.39. If a table of contents is needed, your outline, slightly revised, will serve the purpose.

7.40. Place your completed paper in a folder with a typed label attached giving the title of your paper, your name, name and number of the course, the instructor's name, and the date.
See Nos. 9.17, 9.58.

7.41. Remove from your note cards material you do not use in the paper and keep these extra notes securely bound in a separate pack.

7.42. Save your note cards, because your instructor may wish to examine them.

7.43. If you mount ilustrations in your paper, use rubber cement to prevent wrinkling.

7.44. If tables are to be included in your paper, remember that their only purpose is to communicate ideas, so make them brief and simple.
See No. 7.46.

7.45. Each table should present only one idea.
See No. 7.46.

TABLE I

VIEWING HOURS PER WEEK OF TELEVISION PROGRAMS BY TYPE	
Type	*Hours Per Week*
Audience participation contests	3
Music	5
Panel shows	2
Sports	1
Variety	10
Western movies	3

7.46. Make each table so simple that its meaning is immediately clear to the reader.
See No. 7.45.

7.47. Introduce each table with a brief transitional sentence.

7.48. Number each table consecutively throughout the paper.
Use capital roman numerals.
See No. 7.45.

7.49. Every table must have a simple title which appears in capital letters two spaces under the table number. Do not include as part of the table title words such as "Table Showing."

See No. 7.45.

7.50.   If numbers in the table are rounded off, be sure to inform your reader.

7.51.   If you draw lines in your table, use a ruler with a steel edge, a pen with a fine point, and black ink for greater contrast.

See No. 7.45.

7.52.   Avoid splitting a long table onto two pages. It is better to place it on one page and insert it as close to the contextual matter as possible.

CHAPTER 8

FOOTNOTING

Footnotes add authority to what you say and are a vital part of your paper's documentation. Where they are used, accuracy, completeness, and consistency should prevail.

You will want to refer to Chapter 4 to see how footnote form differs from bibliographic form.

8.1.　Footnotes have two purposes:
　　　a) To provide additional interesting information which is pertinent but not of primary importance.
　　　b) To cite exact page references for quoted matter.
　　　See Sample Term Paper Page 4.

8.2.　Footnotes may be *simple* or *formal,* depending upon the wishes of your instructor, the style followed by your college, and the level of research undertaken in the paper.
　　　See Nos. 8.3 and 8.4.

8.3.　The simplified footnote style merely lists (a) the last name of the author, the title, and the exact page reference, or (b) the title, the reference, and page if the work is anonymous.
　　　　　　　Examples of simple style:
　　　a) [1]Current, *Mr. Lincoln,* p. 382.
　　　b) [2]*The World Book Encyclopedia,* 1982 ed., s.v. Lincoln 12:285–86.
　　　See Term Paper Page 5.

8.4.　The formal footnote style lists the full name (in proper order with family name last), title, place of publication, publisher, date, volume number, and the exact page to which reference is made.

Example of formal footnote style:
[1]Richard N. Current, *Mr. Lincoln* (New York: Dodd, Mead and Co., 1957), p. 382.
See Term Paper Page 2.
See No. 8.15.

8.5. The major purpose of a footnote is to refer the reader to the exact page reference. If your reader is satisfied with this and is content to get more detailed information in the bibliography at the end of the term paper, use the simplified style. If this style is annoying to the reader, use the formal type of footnote. Check with your instructor first.

8.6. A footnote cites the exact page reference, but the bibliography provides complete information about the reference. Every footnote must also have a bibliographic reference.
See Term Paper Page 3 and Bibliography.

8.7. Footnotes are punctuated like sentences. Phrases within them are separated by commas and they end with periods.
See Term Paper Page 3.

8.8. Use formal footnote style when first referring to a work. Later references to the same work may use simplified style.
See Term Paper Pages 3 and 7.

8.9. There are three acceptable methods for numbering footnotes:
a. Continuous numbering throughout the paper
b. Continuous numbering within each chapter
c. Continuous numbering by page with each page starting with number 1.
The sample term paper at the end of this manual follows the style of (a) for footnoting.
Consult your instructor concerning which method to use.

8.10. Place the footnote on the same page as the material being cited.
See Term Paper Page 4.

8.11. If a footnote must be carried over to the next page, break the footnote in the middle of the sentence and complete it at the bottom of the next page in the footnote position. Avoid breaking footnotes.

8.12. The number appearing at the beginning of the footnote is called a footnote number. Although it may be typed on the line, most style manuals suggest its being placed one-half space above the line.
See Term Paper Page 5.

8.13. The footnote number appearing at the end of the matter in the context appears one-half space above the line. This number is the same as the number of the footnote to which it refers at the bottom of the page.
See Term Paper Page 5.

8.14. The first line of the footnote is indented one-half inch from the left margin. All other lines for that footnote are even with the margin.
See Term Paper Page 4.

8.15. Footnotes are single spaced and separated by one blank line.
See Term Paper Page 9.

8.16. There are two ways of separating the text from the foot-notes:
   a. A solid line of underscores 1½ inches long extend-ing from the left margin.
   See Term Paper Page 6.
   b. A solid line of underscores extending from the left margin to the right margin.
   The sample term paper uses the style described in (a).

8.17. Type the line of underscores either for (a) or (b) above, one or two spaces below the last line of context on the page but be consistent. Use the shift and figure 6 keys for making the underscores.
See Term Paper Page 6.

8.18. Allow a minimum of one-half inch (3 lines) for every footnote. This allowance provides for the material as well as for the blank line above and below it.

8.19.   Short cuts may be used to save time when more than one footnote refers to the same work.

The use of the Latin terms, ibid., loc. cit., op. cit., and idem help abbreviate the footnoting task. Such footnotes are used primarily by experienced research writers.

Although there is a trend away from the use of Latin terms in footnoting, you will come upon such terms in your readings, and you should know what they mean. The use of "op. cit." and "loc. cit." is now obsolete. Avoid the over-use of Latin footnotes.
See Abbreviations Section Page 120.

8.20.   Ibid. refers to the immediately preceding footnote. It replaces the author's name and the title when both are the same as in the preceding footnote.
See 8.24 Footnotes 5, 6.
See Term Paper Pages 6, 8, 12.

8.21.   Loc. cit. refers to the same reference. It is used when other footnotes intervene. Loc. cit. is preceded by the author's name. The page number is not given when using loc. cit.
See 8.24 Footnote 9.

8.22.   Op. cit. refers to the work cited earlier. It eliminates the need for the title of the work. The author's name precedes op. cit., and the page reference follows it. Op. cit. is used when there are intervening footnotes. Op. cit. cites the same work but refers to a different page.
See 8.24 Footnote 8.

8.23.   Idem sometimes replaces loc. cit. and op. cit. and means a name previously mentioned. It is used without an underscore or period. Use idem to refer to a previously mentioned name and when a footnote intervenes. However, the use of English rather than Latin is still preferred.
See 8.24 Footnote 10.

8.24.

⁴John Cottrell, *Anatomy of an Assassination* (New York: Funk & Wagnalls, 1966), p. 92.

[5]Ibid.

(Refers to the immediately preceding title and to the same page.)

See Term Paper Page 6.

[6]Ibid., p. 115.

(Refers to the immediately preceding title but to a different page.)

See Term Paper Page 8.

[7]Peter Farb, *Word Play* (New York: Alfred A. Knopf, 1974), p. 79.

[8]Cottrell, *Anatomy*, p. 118. (Simplified footnote style using last name, short title, and page of work cited in footnote 4 but to a *different* page.) Or:

[8]Cottrell, op. cit., p. 118. (Op. cit. may be used when there are intervening footnotes.) The use of op. cit. is discouraged for two reasons:

   a) The name of the work is not given, thus forcing the reader to check back for the title

   b) No space is saved

[9]Farb, *Word Play*, p. 79. (Simplified footnote style instead of loc. cit.) Note that this footnote refers to the work cited in footnote 7 and to the *same* page. Or (but not preferred):

[9]Farb, loc. cit. (Loc. cit. refers to the same work cited in footnote 7 and to the same page.) The use of loc. cit. is discouraged for the same reasons given in 8a and b above.

[10]Cottrell, *Anatomy*, p. 121. (Simplified footnote style shown here refers to Cottrell's book cited in footnote 4 but to a *different* page.) This is the preferred style, but idem may be used when intervening footnotes occur. Or:

[10]Idem, *Anatomy*, p. 121. (Refers to work cited in footnote 4 but to a different page.) Note how idem duplicates what op. cit. and loc. cit. do. However, the simplified footnote style shown immediately above is preferred.

8.25. Common types of footnotes include the following (Italicized words, when typed, are underscored, as are the spaces between the words):

Book

a. Anonymous works
    [1] *Textbooks Are Indispensable!* (New York: The American Textbook Publishers Institute, [n.d.]), p. 32.
b. One author
    William F. Buckley, Jr., *Atlantic High* (Garden City, NY: Doubleday & Company, Inc., 1982), p. 41.
c. Two or three authors
    Steven F. Greenberg and Paul J. Valletutti, *Stress and the Helping Professions* (Baltimore: Paul H. Brookes, 1980), p. 12.
d. More than three authors
    Joe Aberach and others, *Bureaucrats and Politicians in Western Democracies* (Boston: Harvard University Press, 1981), p. 75.
e. Editor as author
    William T. Peck, ed., *Washington's Farewell Address* (New York: The Macmillan Company, 1909), pp. 17–26.
f. Edited by a person other than the author
    William Colburn and Sanford Weinberg, *An Orientation to Listening and Audience Analysis,* ed. by Ronald Applebaum and Roderick Hart (Chicago: Science Research Associates, 1980), p. 288.
g. Edition other than the first
    Clarence Wilbur Taber, *Taber's Cyclopedic Medical Dictionary,* 14th ed. (Philadelphia: F. A. Davis Company, 1981), p. 105.
h. Review
    N. Schedler, review of *Environmental Ethics,* by K. A. Shrader-Prechette, in *Defenders,* August 1982, p. 33.
i. Citing work in more than one volume
    Cyrus Hoy, *Introductions, Notes, and Commentaries to Texts in the Dramatic Works of Thomas Dekker,* vol. 1,

(New York: Cambridge University Press, 1980), pp. 36–39.

Encyclopedia article

j. Author listed
    McGraw-Hill Encyclopedia of Science and Technology, 1977 ed., vol. 12, s.v. "Sensory Learning," by Kao L. Chow.
k. No author listed
    Encyclopedia Americana, 1980 ed., s.v. "Navajo Mountain."

Government document

l. Mary C. Blehar, "Families and Public Policy," *National Institute on Mental Health Monographs.* U.S. Department of Health, Education, and Welfare. (Washington, DC: Government Printing Office, 1979), p. 26.
m. No author listed
    U.S. Department of Commerce, Bureau of the Census, *Statistical Abstract of the United States.* (Washington, DC: Government Printing Office, 1979), p. 321–23.

Newspaper article

n. Author listed
    Paul L. Montgomery, "Garden Plot Is at Center of West Side Fight," *New York Times,* 9 August 1982, Sec. A, p. 1.
o. No author listed
    "Unemployment Soars to Record 9.8 Percent," *Mobile* (AL) *Press-Register,* 7 August 1982, p. 5.
p. Editorial
    "Confusion over Taiwan," Editorial, *Albany* (NY) *Times Union,* 23 August 1982, p. 7.

Periodical or magazine article

q. Author listed
    Rowe Findley, "Our National Forests: Problems in

Paradise," *National Geographic,* 162, September 1982, p. 307.
r. No author listed
"ERA Dies," *Time,* 5 July 1982, p. 29.

Miscellaneous

s. Collected works
Morton N. Cohen, ed., *The Selected Letters of Lewis Carroll* (New York: Pantheon Books, 1982), p. 15.
t. Interview
Interview with Fob James, Governor of Alabama at the Executive Mansion, Montgomery, 1 July 1982.
u. Letter
Letter written by George A. Custer and on file in the National Archives, Washington, DC [n.d.].
v. Pamphlet or Bulletin in a series
United Cerebral Palsy Association, *What Everyone Should Know About Cerebral Palsy* (New York: UCP, Inc., 1977), p. 4.
w. Quarterly
Arthur Burns, "U.S. Relations with West Germany," *The Atlantic Community Quarterly,* 20 (Summer 1982): 153–57.
x. Unpublished doctoral dissertation
Anne F. Roberts, "Library Instruction for Librarians" (D.A. Dissertation, State University of New York at Albany, 1982), p. 15.
y. Translation
Nicholas Yalouris, *Alexander the Great and His Heritage,* trans. David Hardy (Boston: New York Graphic Society, 1980), p. 22.
z. Yearbook article
Marjorie Watson, "Mainstreaming the Educable Mentally Retarded," *Yearbook of Special Education, 1978–79* (Chicago: Marquis Who's Who, Inc., 1978), p. 55.

CHAPTER 9

TYPING THE PAPER

The end is in sight, but don't spoil all you have done by passing in your paper prematurely. Although you may have a very legible handwriting, it is always easier to read from type than from longhand. Besides, the extra effort you exert at this time by getting your paper typed may be reflected in the grade you receive from the person who reads it. Put yourself in the reader's position: Wouldn't you react favorably to a typed paper after "wading" through a number of other papers, many of which may be written in longhand? Do yourself a special favor and submit a clean, attractive, *typed* paper.

9.1. Unless your instructor specifies otherwise, follow the general style suggestions offered in this manual.

9.2. If you plan to bind your paper in a folder, purchase the folder before typing your paper because it will influence the margins you will have.

9.3. Type on white, 8½ - by 11-inch bond, of good quality such as a 20-pound weight having a high rag content. This will give you an attractive, typed copy.

9.4. Type or write on one side of the paper.

9.5. If you handwrite your paper, use white paper with ruled lines approximately one-half inch apart.

9.6. Black ink is preferred when handwriting your paper and when making corrections on the final copy. Make corrections in small print above the line.

9.7. If your final copy has more than two or three errors a

page, write or type the page over to create a more finished effect.

9.8. If someone else is going to type your term paper, go over the handwritten draft with the typist to clarify the spellings of words where your writing may be indistinguishable. This is especially important for quoted matter and footnotes.

9.9. Lend this manual to your typist to use as a guide in typing your paper, paying particular attention to this chapter and also to the sample term paper.

9.10. Retain a carbon copy for your files.

9.11. After inserting the pack (first sheet, carbon, and second sheet) into your typewriter, check to see that it is in proper order.

Peel back the first page. If you see the *dull* side of the carbon, your pack is inserted correctly. Do this every time you insert a new pack.

9.12. After inserting your pack, be sure to remove wrinkles in the carbon paper before typing.

Release the paper release lever by pulling it toward you. The lever is on the right side of the typewriter next to the cylinder knob. Avoid disturbing the pack. Gently run your thumbnail across the paper over the cylinder. Move your paper release back to its original position *away* from you.

9.13. If you type your paper, use a fresh black ribbon to give your paper the best possible appearance.

9.14. Use a cleaning agent (fluid, special putty, or blotters) to clean your typewriter keys. No one likes to read a typed paper in which the individual letters such as *a, o, d, b, c, p,* or *e* are clogged or completely filled because of dirty typewriter bars.

9.15. It makes little difference whether you use an elite- or a pica-style type for your paper. Avoid using script or micro, since they are more difficult to read.

9.16. A typewriter with elite type has a scale just below the cylinder which usually reads from 0 to 130. A pica scale usually reads from 0 to 102. Both machines have 6 lines to the vertical inch. Therefore, a paper 11 inches long has 66 lines.

9.17. If your paper is not going to be enclosed in a folder, use a left margin of 1½ inches and a right margin of one inch. Measure this with a ruler. Place dots at the top of the paper for the left and right margins. Insert your paper into the typewriter and move your marginal stops to the dots.

9.18. If your paper will have a cover, you may need a left margin of two inches.

9.19. To be sure you have enough room for footnotes on your page, follow this procedure:

Immediately after typing the footnote number in your contextual matter, roll down to the one-inch mark at the bottom of your paper. Then roll up three spaces and place a new mark at this point to indicate your last line of contextual matter. Roll up to the contextual matter and continue typing until you come to your second footnote. Follow the same procedure of marking your paper at the bottom by spacing up three more lines from the highest pencil mark.
See No. 8.18.

9.20. On all pages, other than page 1, have a top margin of one inch (six lines). Start typing on the seventh line.
See Term Paper Page 2.

9.21. Set your machine for double spacing. Double spacing means that you have one blank line between every typed line.

9.22. The body of the term paper is double-spaced, but quotations longer than three or four lines, footnotes, and the bibliography are single-spaced. Long quotations and footnotes are indented 5 space from the left margin of the contextual matter. Long quotations are also indented 5 spaces from the right contextual margin.
See Term Paper Page 3.

9.23. If a long quotation takes more than one paragraph, double-space between paragraphs.

9.24.   Underscore words and spaces in book titles.
        See Term Paper Page 13.

9.25.   Titles of articles in periodicals are not underscored but are
        enclosed in quotation marks.
        See No. 8.25 q and r.

9.26.   Double-space between each footnote.
        See Term Paper Page 8.

9.27.   Double-space between each bibliographic entry. If the bib-
        liographic entry requires more than one line, all lines after
        the first are indented 5 spaces.
        See Term Paper Bibliography.

9.28.   It is all right to be one line over or under your bottom
        margin but any more of a variance will result in a "short"
        page or a crowded page.

9.29.   Avoid the use of thesis paper for an undergraduate written
        assignment. The use of such papers may be interpreted as
        putting on "airs." Use plain bond paper.

9.30.   Make underscores according to one of the methods ex-
        plained in number 8.17. Use the shift and the number 6
        keys.

9.31.   Type the line of underscoring either one or two spaces
        below the last line of context on the page but be consistent.
        See Term Paper Page 8.

9.32.   Use the small *l* key for making a figure 1 as in 1983. Your
        typewriter may have a figure 1 key on the top row. If so,
        use it. Do not use the capital I for the figure 1.

9.33.   The title page gives the title of your paper, the word "by,"
        your name, the name of the course, and/or the course
        number, your instructor's name, and the date you submit
        the report, in that order.
        See Term Paper, Title Page.

9.34.   The title is usually typed in capitals on your title page.
        See Term Paper, Title Page.

9.35.   Avoid any decorative designs on the title page.

9.36.   If an outline is to be submitted with the paper, it comes immediately after the title page.
See Chapter 6.

9.37.   The outline is numbered with a small i at the bottom center exactly one inch (6 lines) from the bottom.

9.38.   If your outline requires two pages, the second page is numbered ii at the bottom.

9.39.   The first page of your contextual matter is not numbered, although it does count as page 1. All succeeding pages are numbered in the upper right corner in the same position so that if you were to flip all your numbered pages rapidly, you would see them "dance" before your eyes. Numbers should appear one inch from the right margin, and 3 lines from the top of the paper.
See Term Paper Page 2.

9.40.   If the title of your term paper is also to appear on page 1, place it three inches (18 inches) from the top and center it. If you write your paper, the title appears without underscoring and in small letters. If your paper is typed, the title appears in capitalized form.
See Term Paper Page 1.

9.41.   Space down three lines after the title to begin the first line of your paper.
See Term Paper Page 1.

9.42.   If your paper has paragraph headings, underline the words and spaces.
See Term Paper Page 2.

9.43.   A footnote is preceded by a raised number. This number is the same as the footnote number in the contextual matter on the same page.
See Term Paper Page 11.

9.44.   Footnotes must be double-checked for accuracy because the reader may want to read the exact reference you cite.

9.45. There are three acceptable methods for numbering footnotes.
See No. 8.9.

9.46. Although it is possible to complete a footnote at the bottom of the next page, it is better to retype the page and get the complete footnote on the page where it belongs.

9.47. Indent 5 spaces for the first line of paragraphs and footnotes.
See Term Paper Page 7.

9.48. If you quote poetry, separate it from your text matter by indenting and single spacing it.

9.49. If you include a quotation within a quotation, the inside quotation has single quotation marks while the outside quotation has double quotes.

9.50. Commas and periods appear inside the quotation marks.
See Term Paper Page 9.

9.51. The bibliography constitutes the last page, or pages, of your term paper.
See Term Paper Bibliography.

9.52. Only references that you use in your paper may be included in your bibliography.

9.53. Type the word BIBLIOGRAPHY in capital letters at the top center of the first page on which the bibliography appears.
See Term Paper Bibliography.

9.54. While footnotes have the author's name in signature order, the name is reversed in the bibliography.
See Term Paper Page 2 and Bibliography.

9.55. Arrange your bibliography in alphabetic order.
See Term Paper Bibliography.

9.56. Proofread your final copy.

9.57. If you submit your paper in loose form, without staples or clips, type your name (last name first) in the upper right corner, followed by the page number on each page. Avoid submitting your paper in this form.

9.58. If you submit your paper in a folder, be sure your folder carries a label on the outside.
See No. 7.40.

After completing your term paper, and before submitting it to your instructor, take a few moments to give it a final inspection by using the term paper checklist shown on pages 117–18.

CHAPTER 10

DEVELOPING THE ORAL REPORT

THE PURPOSE OF THIS CHAPTER

This chapter explains how to give an oral report. For reasons of simplicity, the terms oral report, speech, talk, and presentation are used interchangeably even though differences exist. For example, an oral report is the least formal of the three mentioned. A speech is an expression of thoughts in spoken words with little audience participation. A presentation is usually lengthy (one hour or more) and frequently involves the use of audiovisual aids, demonstrations, and audience participation. The key ideas in this chapter should help you prepare and give a short talk, speech, oral report, or presentation. **Before giving your talk, evaluate it by using the Oral Report Checklist on pages 95–98.**

ORAL REPORTING IS AN IMPORTANT SKILL

10.1. It is important for you to be able to speak to groups of people because you will have to do that in whatever career you choose.

10.2. If you can speak effectively before an audience, large or small, your oral communication skills will help you advance in your career.

10.3. Good oral communication skills are in great demand; they are also poorly developed.

DIFFERENCES BETWEEN THE TERM PAPER AND THE ORAL REPORT

10.4. The term paper and the oral report have important differences:

• A term paper transmits the message by written or

typed words. It is read by someone without your being present. Interaction is delayed and when it occurs involves only the reader and the writer.
• An oral report is given to a "live" audience. Interaction is immediate. Rather than one receiver, there may be several or hundreds. Your voice is the communication medium.

10.5. Unlike the term paper, your audience will not know if you can spell the words you are using. Most likely, they *will* know if you are pronouncing them correctly. Grammar, word usage, organization, preparation, and rehearsal are still essential.

WHY GIVE A SPEECH?

10.6. Every speech must have a purpose or there is no reason to give it.

10.7. A speech is usually given to persuade, motivate, instruct, inform, discuss, and recognize (national holiday, important event, etc.).

10.8. Oral reports are given when it is believed that talking to an audience is a better way of transmitting a message than by submitting a written or typed report to be read at a later date and without an immediate exchange of ideas between the sender and the receiver.

WHY SPEECHES FAIL

10.9. Speeches fail because they are poorly organized and lack adequate rehearsal. If you hear a speaker make such statements as "Oh, that reminds me . . ." or "I forgot to mention . . . ," it indicates a weakness in organization and rehearsal effort.

SELECT A TOPIC WITH CARE

10.10. You may be assigned a topic or may have the option of choosing one.
See Chapter 2.

10.11. If you choose a topic, select one that is not offensive, in

good taste, worthy of your time, and makes a positive contribution to the audience.
See Chapter 2.

10.12. Select a topic familiar to you to reduce the time you will need to collect your data.
See Chapter 2.

10.13. If your topic is noncontroversial, use a direct approach. Here, you first explain your point of view, follow with facts, provide a rationale, and conclude with a summary.

10.14. If your topic is controversial, organize your speech by beginning with facts, followed by a rationale, and concluding with your value judgments and/or recommendations, if appropriate.
See No. 10.96.

10.15. It is better to discuss only one or two points in a speech than to try to cover the entire topic.

How Much Should a Speaker Know About the Topic?

10.16. A good speaker should be as knowledgeable as possible about the topic. This does not mean one is expected to know all there is to know about the subject to be discussed. There are many subjects about which little is known; however, these topics can still be developed into oral reports with some research effort.

10.17. The most difficult thing to do when given an assignment is to get started. Do not procrastinate.

10.18. Establish target dates for the following:

Month   Day

_____ _____ Identify the topic
_____ _____ Write a clear statement of the purpose of the talk
_____ _____ Research the topic
_____ _____ Develop an outline
_____ _____ Write the draft
_____ _____ Edit and type the draft

_____ _____ Edit and type the *final* copy
_____ _____ Rehearse the oral report
_____ _____ Give the oral report

10.19. The following chart should help you complete your assignment:

Choose a topic
↓
Analyze the audience
↓
Gather the data
↓
Prepare your outline
↓
Write the draft
↓
Edit your draft
↓
Type your second draft or final copy
↓
Tape your edited final copy
↓
Decide whether to read your speech or use note cards
↓
Rehearse your oral report
↓
Visit the room where you will give your talk
↓
Determine your equipment needs
↓
Decide on audio-visuals and demonstrations
↓
Give your presentation

ANALYZE THE AUDIENCE

10.20. Try to get the answers to these important questions:
- Who is my audience?
- How much do they know about the topic?
- If they do not have much knowledge about the topic, what words shall I use that will clearly express my thoughts (avoiding difficult and technical terms)?
- If they have expressed an opinion about the topic, what is it?
- Why should the audience be interested in my topic? (A vested interest, perhaps? If so, discover what it is!)
- What is the size of the group? (Large, small, etc.)
- What is their age range? (16–18; 25–60, etc.)
- What are their attitudes about the topic? Friendly? Hostile? Apathetic? Empathetic?
- What will be the mix of males and females?
- What is the audience's educational level? (high school, etc.)
- What effect do I want my talk to have on the audience?
- What strategy will I need to follow to accomplish the purpose of my talk?
- Will a question-and-answer period be appropriate?

GATHER YOUR DATA

10.21. Review Chapters 3 and 5 on using the library and taking notes.

10.22. Collect more data than you need. This will help you if you have a question and answer period following your talk.
See Nos. 10.111–10.116.

10.23. Use 3- by 5-inch index cards or paper cut to size to collect your data, holding them horizontally.
See Nos. 5.5, 5.6, 5.7.

10.24. Place only one fact on each card or paper, using one side only. If you need more writing space, go to a second card or paper and use a numbering system to link both such as 1A, 1B.
See No. 5.10.

10.25. Use the reverse side to cite the data source in case you need to verify some fact.
See No. 5.2.

10.26. Save all note cards for possible future referral.

PREPARE YOUR OUTLINE

10.27. Prepare an outline from your note cards by arranging them in some logical order.
See Chapter 6.

10.28. The arrangement of your outline is determined by the strategy you will use in presenting your topic to the audience.
See Nos. 10.20, 10.29, 10.30, 10.31, 10.32.

THE TYPICAL SPEECH HAS THREE PARTS

10.29. Speeches usually include introductory comments that set the theme for the talk, followed by the body where the main points are developed, and concluding with a summary and/or recommendations, if appropriate.

THE OPENING AND CLOSING SHOULD BE DYNAMIC

10.30. Your opening remarks need to gain immediate audience attention; otherwise, they will listen for a short while and then turn their attention elsewhere. A good way to attract attention is to ask a question or display some object for their viewing.

10.31. Gain the audience's attention but avoid startling dramatics that may frighten or alarm them.

10.32. The opening and closing must support each other and both must capture the interest of the audience.

WRITE THE DRAFT

10.33. Be generous in your use of action verbs for they are more interesting than are the passive type.
See No. 7.9.

10.34. Avoid passive verbs. (Example: "It is appreciated ..."—Say, "I appreciate...")

10.35. The simple sentence having a subject, verb, and object is easy to write and easy to understand.

10.36. Use adjectives and adverbs carefully as they may be interpreted differently.

10.37. Give special attention to grammar, sentence structure, and transitional devices. (Examples of transitions: "On the other hand ...", "My second point is ...", "But ...") Transitions help achieve forward movement by keeping your audience with you on the point you are discussing.

10.38. Avoid unnecessary words. (Example: "I would like to take this opportunity to thank you for ..." when "Thank you for ..." is more to the point.)

10.39. Use paragraph headings and underline them. When reading a typed speech from 8½- by 11-inch white paper, the paragraph headings may be all you need to discuss the content of the paragraph without having to read every word.
See Sample Term Paper Page 2.

EDIT YOUR DRAFT

10.40. After putting your draft aside for a day or two, edit it. In the editing process, you will do some or all of the following:
   • Underline words you want to emphasize.
   • Write reminders to yourself at appropriate places. (Examples: Pause here, look at audience, display object.)

- Delete Latin terms and trite expressions. (Examples: *modus operandi,* "Be that as it may.") They are not always understood or appeciated.
- Avoid slang expressions.
- Refrain from using words that may convey different meanings. (Examples: *bread*—money, food; *pad*—writing tablet, bed.)
- Eliminate duplication of thoughts.
- Reduce the use of "which" and "that."
- Maintain an average sentence length of 15–19 words.
- Avoid sexist language (Example: The manager spoke to *his* staff.") Some managers are women!
- Put people into your speech by using names.
- Avoid stilted and impersonal language. (Example: "It behooves me to say . . ." and "It has been said . . ." when "I would like to say . . ." and "We often hear it said that . . ." is better.)

Type Your Second Draft or Final Copy

10.41. Review Chapter 9, especially Nos. 9.3, 9.4, 9.13, 9.14, 9.56.

10.42. Use the largest type size available. If only elite or pica size is available, type the speech using all capital letters for easy reading.
See No. 9.16.

10.43. Have 1½-inch left and right margins.

10.44. Have one-inch top and bottom margins.

10.45. Triple-space throughout but leave four single spaces between paragraphs.

10.46. Type page numbers on all pages.
See No. 9.39.

10.47. Try to end a paragraph on a page rather than continuing onto another page and thus avoid the need to carry over a thought.

Tape Your Edited Final Copy

10.48. After your speech has been edited, dictate it into a tape recorder.

See No. 10.49 before doing this.

10.49. Speak at about 120 words a minute. Here is how you can do this:

With your typed speech in front of you, mark off 30 words and place a diagonal mark at that place; do the same after every 30 words. Now, using a watch with a second hand, begin dictating (practice first) your speech to arrive at the first diagonal in 15 seconds. Continue dictating to arrive at the second diagonal mark in another 15 seconds. Do the same for each group of 30 words. At this rate, you will be speaking at 120 words a minute. Note this example of inserting diagonal marks:

Lincoln's Assassination—A Murder Mystery

The purpose of this presentation is to point out some of the mysteries surrounding the tragic death of President Abraham Lincoln. The murder of this great man is considered to/be one of the greatest tragedies befalling the American people. Another tragedy stemming from the murder is the apparent breakdown of jurisprudence which took place following the killing. With each/passing year, the murder plot and subsequent assassination become more dimmed and the circumstances of the conspiracy, the act itself, and the trial are now hidden among a maze of/abstractions and generalities with each writer's interpretation of the tragedy connected with the President.

This marking method will also help you estimate with some accuracy the length of your talk. Determine the total number of words in your speech and divide by 120. If your speech, for example, contains 1,200 words, and you speak at 120 words a minute, your speech is 10 minutes long.

10.50. Now that you know the length of your talk, in its present form, you may have to shorten or lengthen it to keep within the time allowance given you. If shortening is needed, look for ways of removing parts of your speech that may be interesting but not necessary. If lengthening is needed, go back to your research note cards. *See Nos. 5.5, 10.26.* Look for additional data you have not used and see where it might be inserted into your talk.

10.51. With your final edited copy before you, repeat No. 10.48.

10.52. Listen to the tape recording, paying close attention to diction, pronunciations, voice emphasis, tonal qualities, and speed. The way you use your voice (strategic pauses and higher and lower tones) provides the punctuation for your speech.

10.53. Pronounce all word endings and syllables. (Examples: say swimmin*g* instead of swimmin; say particu*lar*ly instead of particuly.)

10.54. Avoid regional accents. Emulate news commentators you hear on the radio and TV for their speech is free of regional accents. A listener usually cannot get a clue as to their country or origin or where they call "home" in the United States.

10.55. Determine if there is a sincere and confident quality to your speech. Does it sound like you? Does it carry conviction?

10.56. If you have stumbled over the pronunciations of words, substitute easier ones. A thesaurus will help.

10.57. Have someone listen to your tape and evaluate it.

10.58. As you listen to the tape, follow along in your typed speech and underline words you want to emphasize.

DECIDE WHETHER TO READ YOUR SPEECH OR
USE NOTE CARDS

10.59. Do not attempt to memorize your speech. The most experienced speakers are sometimes at a loss for words because of a memory gap.

10.60. If you are a novice at giving speeches, follow the advice of professional speakers. They recommend that you read your speech, making sure it is done in a way that maintains interest and eye-to-eye contact with the audience.

10.61. Whether you plan to read your speech or use note cards, rehearse, rehearse, rehearse!
        See No. 10.64.

10.62. If you decide to use note cards, use either the 3- by 5- or 5- by 8-inch size. Print the key ideas using a black felt marking pen. Do not use complete sentences. Print is more legible than handwriting. Hold the cards vertically.

10.63. Number each card in the upper right-hand corner. Staple all cards in the upper left corner. If the cards are accidentally dropped during your talk, they can be recovered without having to be put back into their proper order. Do the same if using a typed speech.

REHEARSE YOUR ORAL REPORT

10.64. Get enthused about giving your talk. Getting "psyched up" helps reduce tension, stress, and anxiety concerning your attitudes toward your talk. Consider this:
    • You have researched your topic.
    • You know more about your topic than does the audience.
    • You are prepared to answer questions because you have collected more data than you need.
    • You have rehearsed so much that you are completely familiar with your speech.

10.65. When you rehearse, do all of the following:
    • Have an audience even if it is only a vacant chair or one person.
    • Stand in front of a full-length mirror to observe your body movements (keep them to a minimum).

• Have a platform for your typed speech or note cards (table, stack of books, box, etc.).
• Keep one finger on the line of your typed speech as you read it to avoid losing your place.
• Look at your audience as much as possible.
• Use a pleasant, nonthreatening voice with strategic pauses, proper emphasis, and changes in speed.
• Rehearse enough times to become thoroughly acquainted with your speech and thus increase your ability to maintain eye contact with the audience.

VISIT THE ROOM WHERE YOU WILL GIVE YOUR TALK

10.66. The physical setting where you will give your talk is important and you should visit it and make note of the following:

• Does the room have windows? Try to get a room with windows and chairs that face away from the outside light.
• Where are the wall electrical outlets located? Are they where you need them if using equipment powered by electricity (slide or film projector)?
• Can the outlets receive a three-prong plug? If not, you will probably need an adapter as most electrically operated viewing machines have a three-prong plug. A hardware store sells adapters.
• What are the seating arrangements? Are they tablet-arm chairs? Auditorium type seats? Are the seats fixed or movable? Are they facing the direction you desire? Will someone rearrange them for you if you wish?
• Are the windows equipped with curtains or shades? Do the windows open? Do the curtains and shades work?
• What instructional (audiovisuals, chalkboard, easel, etc.) equipment is in the room? Does the room have a screen for viewing slides or films? Do you know how to operate the equipment you will use

in your presentation? If not, have someone instruct you.

• Does the room have light switches? Where, and how many? Is it possible to turn off *some* but not *all* of the lights? (Avoid showing an image on a screen in total darkness because people cannot take notes, and might trip over electrical wires or people if they do not remain in their chairs.)

• Will there be noises or distractions over which you have no control such as road repairs, building construction? If so, this may influence the way you want the seats to face or your choice of room.

DETERMINE YOUR EQUIPMENT NEEDS

10.67. Now that you have visited the room where you will give your presentation, you know what equipment is available or what you will need:

(Check what you need)

Chalkboard _____

Eraser _____

Chalk _____

Screen _____

Easel and pad _____

Film projector (16 mm?) _____

Slide projector (carousel type?) _____

Adapter for a three-prong plug _____

Lectern equipped with lighting device _____

Pointer _____

Microphone _____

Extension cord _____

Marking pen (felt tip) _____

10.68. Arrange to have whatever equipment and supplies you need available when you give your presentation.

PREPARE YOUR AUDIOVISUALS AND DEMONSTRATIONS

10.69. When properly used, slides, films, drawings, illustrations, chalkboard notes, and easel pad sketches can be effective.

10.70. Avoid freehand drawings. Prepare beforehand, if possible.

10.71. Visuals should be simple, few in number, carefully and accurately made, easy to understand, and large enough for all to see.

10.72. Each visual on a screen should be supported by a prepared text written on an index card.

10.73. Charts are best prepared on one-inch grid paper. A 27-by 32½-inch easel pad sheet (50 sheets to a pad) and marked off in light blue square inches is ideal. The grid allows you to draw straight lines and helps achieve proportional accuracy in charts such as column diagrams and graphs.

10.74. Demonstrations are more effective when there is audience participation. Arrange for a "volunteer" beforehand.

10.75. If using an easel, put penciled notes, lightly printed, on the left side of the easel pad sheet. This is your script and it cannot be seen by the audience and thus frees you from referring to notes that are hand-held.

10.76. A pointer, rather than a finger, is preferred when calling attention to something being projected on a screen or written on an easel pad sheet and does not get in the way of the audience's view.

YOUR APPEARANCE IS IMPORTANT

10.77. Before entering the room where you will give your talk, view yourself in a mirror. Hair combed? Face, hands, and fingernails clean? Tie straight? Trousers arranged properly? Makeup on as it should be?

10.78. Whatever you wear should be clean, without rips or missing buttons.

10.79. Minimize wearing jewelry. A simple necklace, bracelet, earrings, ring, and watch are suitable for female speakers. Male speakers may properly wear a ring and watch. Anything more might distract the audience.

10.80. Avoid being over or under dressed. If you know the audience, dress appropriately.

YOUR RAPPORT WITH THE AUDIENCE MUST BE POSITIVE

10.81. Avoid trying to flatter your audience. (Examples: "I'm honored to be your speaker" or "I feel humble talking to this group.") It does not sound sincere.

10.82. Never apologize to your audience. (Example: "I haven't had time to properly prepare my talk" or "I'm not the best qualified to speak on this subject" or "A coin was tossed as to who would be your speaker and you got me—sorry about that.")

10.83. Do not end your presentation by thanking the audience. When your presentation has ended, pick up your notes and return to your seat.

GIVE THE PRESENTATION

10.84. If your voice is soft, speak louder than usual.

10.85. If you need to remind yourself to speak to be heard, write the word LOUD on an index card and keep it alongside your notes or typed speech as you address the audience.

10.86. If you use a microphone, speak from 6 to 12 inches away from it. Practice beforehand and learn how to turn it on and off and how to raise and lower it.

10.87. Hold your body movements to a minimum and stand in a relaxed posture.

10.88. Avoid finger pointing and table pounding as a form of emphasis as these are threatening and upsetting gestures.

10.89. Place both hands on the lectern and leave them there.

10.90. Refrain from running your hands through your hair,

tossing your hair to keep it out of your eyes (use pins), scratching, rubbing your nose, or clearing your throat, as these are signs of tension and stress.

10.91. Tension and stress are normal and serve to remind speakers to be prepared. Thus, both tension and stress can be viewed as helpful. Adequate rehearsal reduces tension and stress.

10.92. Avoid the use of crude, vulgar, and obscene language.

10.93. If a noise (passing motorist, airplane, etc.) occurs while you are speaking, remain silent until the noise stops. Do not compete with it by shouting to be heard. (This also gives you a little rest break.)

10.94. Observe the audience as you talk. If they look confused about something you have said, rephrase it for better understanding.

10.95. Have a contingency (backup) plan ready in case you are unable to be heard (outside noises) or seen (evening power failure). Plan what to do in such an eventuality.

10.96. If your topic is controversial or one in which you have an unpopular opinion, keep your emotions under control and do not try to *tell* your audience anything. Plan your strategy for getting them to accept your viewpoint. *See No. 10.14.*

10.97. Be yourself. The audience will know if you are putting on "airs."

10.98. Avoid the common tendency to use such expressions as "You know," "Okay," and "Uh-huh."

10.99. Inform the audience of how long you will speak. If they don't wonder, their attention may not wander!

10.100. To prevent exceeding your time allowance, arrange beforehand for someone in the front row to give you a two-minute warning signal indicating that you have two minutes left in your speech.

10.101. A short talk does not require a rest break—longer ones do. A one-hour presentation (or longer) will generate audience restlessness and a rest break will be needed. Either have them stand for a stretch (without leaving their seating area) or give them a ten-minute break. Letting them leave the room is risky; some people will not return, others will delay their return and arrive back in the room when you are speaking and be a distraction. Use good judgment.

10.102. During your talk, watch the audience for signs of boredom, confusion, inattentiveness, etc. If you feel you are losing their interest, you can regain it by asking direct and indirect questions:
   • Direct—(Select someone from the audience). Look at that person and ask a nonthreatening, easy-to-answer question that has some relationship to your immediate statements. (Example: "Alice, if you have heard of the term acid rain, please tell us what that term means to you"—where the subject being discussed deals with pollution.)
   • Indirect—(Look at audience but at no one in particular). Ask a question designed to regain their attention. (Example: "What do you think of the idea of finding water with a forked stick?"—where the subject is water dowsing.)

TELLING JOKES AND FUNNY STORIES CAN BE RISKY

10.103. In general, avoid telling jokes and funny stories.

10.104. A joke is appropriate only when it has some relationship to the topic.

10.105. If you plan to tell a joke, do not preface it by saying "This reminds me of a story . . ." Use an opening statement that leads normally into the joke.

10.106. Some stories and jokes are always inappropriate because they are insulting, crude, offensive, and without merit. Use good judgment.

10.107. A serious topic need not be *deadly* serious. Humor, properly used, can keep the speech from being dull.

10.108. Long presentations should be supported by some change in activity such as looking at an object, asking questions, etc., to maintain interest and reduce audience fatigue.

USE HANDOUT MATERIALS JUDICIOUSLY

10.109. Handout materials, if used, should be few in number, simple in design, and easy to understand.

10.110. Have someone distribute your handout materials and let them know when you want them to do this.

PREPARE FOR A QUESTION-AND-ANSWER PERIOD

10.111. If you know the answer to a question, give a simple, brief response to avoid using up valuable time for other questions.

10.112. Avoid asking questions that can be answered with "Yes" or "No," or "I don't know."
See No. 10.102.

10.113. Reduce the risk of not being able to answer questions by adequately researching your topic.

10.114. If the audience asks questions, consider it a compliment because it means they have been listening.

10.115. If you don't know the answer to a question, admit it. Don't fake an answer. The most experienced speakers get questions they cannot answer. Either say, "I don't know," or promise to get the answer to them as soon as possible.

10.116. Have several blank index cards with you for writing questions for which you don't have immediate answers. Note who asked the question. Obtain the answer as soon as possible and give it to that person.

KEEP SPEECH, EVALUATE AND REVISE IT

10.117. Retain your typed speech or notes and your research

cards; you may be asked to present it to another audience.

10.118. At the top left corner of the first page, indicate the following:
- Date on which you gave the presentation
- The audience (identify by name and city)
- The number of minutes you spoke
- Number of words in your typed speech
- The questions, if any, asked by the audience
- Your own evaluation of the effectiveness of your speech (good, fair)

10.119. While your oral report is fresh in your mind, write suggestions about how it could be improved, if given again.

10.120. Locate the sections in your speech where challenges came from the audience. Review your data to eliminate future challenges.

10.121. Review the Oral Report Checklist on pages 95–98 and evaluate your speech.

10.122. Use this checklist *before* and *after* your oral presentation.

ORAL REPORT CHECKLIST

1. Have I examined the term paper checklist on pages 117–18 as a means of improving the quality of my typed speech (not all items are appropriate)?   ___ ___

2. If speaking from note cards, are my key words underlined and in large print for easy reading?   ___ ___

3. Are my note cards or typed speech numbered and stapled to prevent a "disaster" if they are accidentally dropped during my presentation?   ___ ___

4. Have I used a new black ribbon on the typewriter, and are the type bars clean?   ___ ___

5. Have I typed on white 8½- by 11-inch paper of heavy weight (20- or 24-pound)?   ___ ___

6. Is my speech typed in all capitals for easy reading?   ___ ___

7. Have I used triple spacing in the body of the speech and left four single lines between paragraphs?   ___ ___

8. Have I analyzed my audience—their interests, points of view, knowledge of the topic, educational level, etc.?   ___ ___

9. Does my speech have a definite purpose or message?   ___ ___

10. Have I planned my strategy for making an effective presentation?   ___ ___

11. Have I identified what I want my audience to gain from my oral report?   ___ ___

12. Do I maintain good eye contact with my audience?   ___ ___

continued on next page

Yes No

13. Do I keep their attention from wandering by asking direct and/or indirect (overhead) questions? ____ ____

14. Am I watching for signals from my audience such as confusion and, if so, am I prepared to rephrase for better understanding? ____ ____

15. Do I feel that my talk will be favorably received? ____ ____

16. During my editing, did I weed out unnecessary words and jargon, and refrain from using words that have unclear meanings? ____ ____

17. Does my voice sound convincing, interesting, and sincere as I listen to it on the tape recorder? ____ ____

18. Do I project my voice in a way to show enthusiasm and confidence? ____ ____

19. Is my voice loud enough for all to hear? ____ ____

20. Does my opening statement capture the attention of the audience? ____ ____

21. Have I waited until I have my audience's attention before speaking? ____ ____

22. Is my talk interesting? ____ ____

23. Do I begin with an interesting opening, move to the main points, and close with a logical conclusion that supports my facts? ____ ____

24. Can my talk be given within the time allowance set for it? ____ ____

25. Am I speaking at about 120 words a minute? ____ ____

26. Have I done enough research on the topic to be able to handle questions from the audience with ease? ____ ____

27. Do I use transitional terms such as "My second point . . .", "On the other hand . . .", and "To summarize . . ." to keep my audience thinking along with me? ____ ____

28. Have I rehearsed enough times so that I can

continued on next page

Yes No

give the talk with minimum reliance on my
notes or typed speech?

29. Have I tape-recorded my talk and listened
    carefully to my voice, word choice, usage,
    volume, and inflection?

30. Have I changed words I stumbled over during
    rehearsal to words that convey the same
    meaning but are easier to pronounce?

31. Do I keep my hands motionless and on the
    lectern?

32. Do I keep my body movements to a mini-
    mum?

33. Do I refrain from distracting the audience by
    not picking lint off my clothing, by not
    clearing my throat, by not rubbing my nose,
    etc.?

34. Do I use correct grammar and is it free of
    slang and trite expressions?

35. Have I checked my appearance in a mirror
    just prior to addressing the audience?

36. Do I appear poised and confident in front of
    the audience?

37. Do I remember to smile occasionally while I
    am speaking?

38. Do I remember to look around the room as I
    talk, focusing my eyes first on one person
    for awhile and then on another as a way
    of keeping their attention and showing in-
    terest in them?

39. Am I familiar with the operation of the equip-
    ment I plan to use in my presentation?

40. Are my visual aids well made, simple in de-
    sign, large enough to see, and clearly visible
    to all in the room?

41. Do I have a contingency (backup) plan ready
    in case something unexpected happens dur-
    ing my talk (power failure, no lights, etc.)?

continued on next page

Each of the above questions should be answered with a "Yes." If you have answered "No" to any of them, go back to that particular section of your presentation because it may need improvement.

HOW TO USE THIS SAMPLE
TERM PAPER

As you will see, the numbers of the key ideas that appear in the text have been noted on the sample term paper. You may easily look up the explanation or the reason for the use of a particular form by turning back from the sample paper to the specific item in the text.

For example, **7.3** on the sample title page of the term paper refers you back to Chapter 7, Item 3 or 7.3.

9.34   9.33

LINCOLN'S ASSASSINATION--A MURDER MYSTERY

7.3

7.38

Leave one blank line here ———————→   by

Gerald Driscoll

English 100A

Dr. Susan M. Boone

May 1, 19--

↑

1½ inches

9.40

LINCOLN'S ASSASSINATION--A MURDER MYSTERY

9.41

The purpose of this paper is to point up some of
the mysteries surrounding the tragic death of President
Abraham Lincoln. The murder of this great man is considered to be one of the greatest tragedies befalling the
American people. Another tragedy stemming from the murder
is the apparent breakdown of jurisprudence and American
justice which took place following the killing. With
each passing year, the murder plot and subsequent
assassination become more dimmed and the circumstances
of the conspiracy, the act itself, and the trial are now
hidden among a maze of abstractions and generalities with
each writer's interpretation of the tragedy connected
with the President. In fact, a perusal of any number of
books on the subject reveals inconsistencies, gaps,
confusions, and widely differing opinions on the events
leading up to and following the killing. This term paper
will include official government evidence and will attempt
to present facts rather than fiction about Lincoln's murder.

It is common knowledge that John Wilkes Booth killed
Lincoln, but the part played by those who went on trial
for their lives as accomplices in the atrocious crime is
still clouded in a veil of mystery.

9.20   9.39   2

This paper will pinpoint certain events connected
with the assassination--events that to this day contribute
to the fact that President Lincoln's assassination is
indeed a murder mystery.

9.42 Lincoln's premonition of death

The years have not unfolded the reason why Lincoln
acted so strangely on the day he was shot. He appeared
to be extremely melancholy and expressed the fear that
men were attempting to do him harm. In fact, when leaving
the White House for Ford's Theatre, he said "good-bye"
rather than his customary "good night" to his servant.
This attitude of impending disaster and other statements
made by Lincoln lead one to wonder from what source his
fears originated. He took a fatalistic view of a possible
assassination, however, when he said, "No use worrying.
What is to be, must be. If anyone is really determined to
kill me, I shall be killed!"[1]

10.39 Lack of adequate protection provided for the President

It would almost appear that Lincoln never had a chance
to escape from death the night of April 14. Four instances
will illustrate this. First, Mrs. Lincoln dismissed the
regular guard and had requested that the President's life
be protected by a metropolitan policeman by the name of
Parker. It must be assumed that Mrs. Lincoln did not know

9.54 ———————
       [1]Richard N. Current, Mr. Lincoln (New York: Dodd,
8.4 Mead and Co., 1957), p.382.

that Parker had a reputation for drunkenness while on
duty, of conduct unbecoming an officer, and of leaving
his post without proper authority.[2] In fact, protective
measures to guard the life of the President were
criminally negligent. Second, the armed guard Parker,
whom Mrs. Lincoln had requested and whose duty it was to
stand outside the presidential box and "screen" all passers-
by, was mysteriously absent from his post at the time Booth
made his fateful entry. Third, no one had bothered to
notice the peephole in the door that Booth had bored on
the morning of the murder. Fourth, the broken lock on the
door of the presidential box had not been repaired. Into
all these errors, omissions, and faulty security measures
did the President of the United States walk.

> On the night of April 14, 1865, he [Lincoln]   **5.27**
> **9.22** attended a performance of <u>Our American Cousin</u> at
> Ford's Theatre in Washington. A few minutes
> after 10 o'clock, a shot rang through the crowded
> house. John Wilkes Booth, one of the best-known
> actors of the day, had shot the President in the
> head from the back of the Presidential box.[3]

This tragedy gave rise to even more tragedies and set off
one of the most mixed-up manhunts and criminal trials ever
to be conducted anywhere.

8.6 ————————————————   **8.8**

[2]Otto Eisenschiml, <u>Why Was Lincoln Murdered?</u> (New
8.7 York: Grosset and Dunlap, 1937), pp. 12, 14.

4.11   [3]<u>The World Book Encyclopedia</u>, 1982 ed., s.v. Lincoln
12:285-6

After shooting Lincoln,[4] Booth jumped from the
presidential box onto the stage, catching his right spur
in the U. S. Treasury flag. This unforeseen accident was
to implicate and ruin the life of one Dr. Samuel Mudd,
physician, who at this moment may very well have been
completely unaware of Booth's intentions or activities.[5]
We will speak more of Dr. Mudd later.

Booth's change of plans from kidnaping to murder

John Wilkes Booth was a nationally-known actor and
the grandson of a man who helped runaway slaves escape.
John Wilkes was unlike his grandfather in that he (John)
was a strong southern sympathizer. Kelly makes an
interesting statement regarding Booth's motives in the
crime when he says:

> Which of the shadows hid the demoniacal
> movements of the man who cast himself in the
> role of the villain in the arch tragedy of his   8.10
> own authorship that night, remains a mystery.[6]

Booth, the idol of the American stage, was a strange
and vain man indeed. His income amounted to over $20,000
a year, and he had everything he could possibly want,
except perhaps undying fame as the executioner of a "tyrant,"

8.1 [4] A single-shot, muzzle-loading, .41-caliber Derringer
pistol was used.

8.1 [5] U. S. Dept. of the Interior, Lincoln Museum and the
House Where Lincoln Died, Booklet, reprint (Washington, DC:
1956), p. 14.

8.14 [6] Edward James Kelly, The Crime at Ford's Theatre
(Washington, DC: Government Service, Inc., Action Publishers,
1944), p. 4.
8.10

as he viewed Lincoln. Contrary to popular belief, he originally had intended to kidnap the President and exchange him for southern prisoners of war. The extent of southern losses, however, changed Booth's mind about the practicability of such a move, and in its place another plan had to be developed. The resulting trial and historical accounts of the incident have never made clear whether or not the persons convicted of the crime of being accessories knew of Booth's change of plans from kidnaping to murder.

Booth's decision to kill the President may have resulted from Lincoln's statement of April 12,[7] that he (Lincoln) hoped that the freed slaves of Louisiana would be given the right to vote. Kelly remarked that when Booth heard of this, he fumed loudly and said, "Now, by God, I'll put him through!"[8] 8.13

General Grant's strange behavior

Now let us consider General Grant for a moment. The evening at Ford's Theatre was to honor Lincoln as well as Grant and, unbeknown to either of them, both men had been marked for murder by Booth. Lincoln had asked the general and his wife to join the presidential party. "Earlier in the morning, General and Mrs. Grant had accepted an invitation from the President to accompany

---

8.12 [7]During the closing days of the war in 1865.
8.13 [8]Kelly, The Crime, p. 4.

8.3

him and Mrs. Lincoln to the theatre."[9]

7.28   History has never satisfactorily explained why the general and his lady suddenly notified the President on the same afternoon of that terrible day that they would be unable to attend the performance. With this abrupt explanation, the Grants boarded the train and headed for New Jersey to visit their children who were attending a camp.[10] **7.26**

7.28   Lincoln invited several other people to attend in place of the Grants but all declined. Finally, the President was able to get a Miss Clara Harris, a daughter of a senator, and her escort, a Major Henry R. Rathbone, to join him in the presidential box. Does it not seem strange that the President of the United States had great difficulty in obtaining guests for the evening's performance of what was to be a gala affair?

7.28   Grant's behavior in his refusal to attend was indeed strange. Only sixteen months later during the presidency of Andrew Johnson, Grant accepted another invitation to attend a reception at the Executive Mansion because he considered such an invitation from the President to be tantamount to an order, and Grant had always prided himself by saying he never disobeyed an order. One must question why Grant did not consider Lincoln's invitation to be an

8.16 _____ **8.17**

[9]_Lincoln Museum and the House Where Lincoln Died_, p. 6.

8.24 8.20 [10]Ibid.

7.26

order but did feel the need to obey the invitation of
Johnson.

Stanton's famous last words about Lincoln

The dastardly deed had been done. Booth carried out
his promise to "put him (Lincoln) through," for on the
morning of April 15, the President died. An untold number
of accounts quote Stanton, Secretary of War, as saying,
"Now he belongs to the ages" at the moment of Lincoln's
death. Yet it is quite likely that this famous eulogy was
never spoken by Stanton or by anyone else. Witnesses present
at Lincoln's death later recount many versions of what
Stanton was supposed to have said:

> Now he belongs to the angels
> Now he belongs to history
> And now he belongs to the ages
> Doctor, please lead in prayer /note the lack
> of any reference to the "ages" saying 7
> Ah dear friend! there is none now to do me
> justice; none to tell the world of the
> anxious hours we have spent together!
> There lies the most perfect ruler of men the
> world has ever seen.[11]

Booth's escape into Maryland

And what of Booth all this time? He was suffering
from the effects of a broken leg received in his fall to
the stage. But let us retrace his steps.

Booth, considering himself to be a national hero
now that he had rid the country of a "tyrant," made his

8.8   [11]Eisenschiml, Lincoln Murdered, pp. 482-84.

escape from the theater by horseback and approached the
sentry at the Navy Yard Bridge. From this point on,
history disagrees on what took place. One historical
account states that Booth passed himself off as a Maryland
planter from "near Beantown." [12] The sentry, Sergeant
Silas T. Cobb, violated orders by allowing Booth to pass
through the gate after curfew. Eisenschiml's account of
the incident differs widely from Kelly's:

> A Sergeant Cobb, who was in charge at
> the north end of the bridge, had questioned
> Booth and, after a brief conversation, had
> let him pass . . . 5.24
>
> 5.26 . . . .
> It is characteristic of Booth that he
> did not hesitate to give his true name to the
> sentinel at the bridge, for, in the fantastic
> mind of the assassin, his act was to be the
> perfect crime of the ages, and he the most
> heroic assassin of all times! [13] 7.19
>
> . . . .
> To return to Sergeant Cobb, one can
> understand his decision to let Booth . . . 5.24
> pass unconditionally. . . . He /Cobb_/ had to
> make his decisions, and he made them accord-
> ing to his best judgment. On what grounds can
> it be explained, however, that having heard
> Booth's name from his own lips, this soldier
> did not give the alarm as soon as the news of
> Lincoln's assassination reached him? [14]

Cobb's failure to mention Booth's passing through his
post was never brought up in the trial. Strange indeed
that not one of the prosecuting officers asked

9.31

9.26 [12]Kelly, The Crime, p. 15.
7.19 8.24 [13]Eisenschiml, Lincoln Murdered, pp. 107-109.
8.24 8.20 [14]Ibid., pp. 108-109.

this guard why he, Cobb, never reported that Booth
headed into Maryland.

Confusion rose to new heights in the hours immediately following Booth's cowardly shot. To cite one
illustration, the New York Herald carried news dispatches
in every edition. In the rush to get out its first
extra on the slaying, the Herald misdated its paper by
carrying the date Friday, April 14, on its masthead.[15]

Secretary of War Stanton's unexplained silence

A second strange event concerns the actions of the
Secretary of War, Edwin Stanton. Rather than following
the most logical course of action by releasing the name
of the assassin to the newspapers as soon as possible as
an aid in Booth's apprehension, Stanton withheld the
name until several hours after the crime had been committed.
A news dispatch of 1:30 a.m. appearing in the Herald
dated April 15 states "some evidence of the guilt of the 7.21
party who attacked the President is in the possession
of the police."[16] 9.50

The cloud of suspicion over Dr. Samuel Mudd

What was Booth doing during the hours immediately
following the shooting? He had made a safe escape into
Maryland although racked by pain from a broken leg bone.
Because the home of Dr. Samuel Mudd, a general practitioner,

----

[15]The true date was Saturday, April 15. New York
8.15 Herald, Whole No. 10,456.

[16]The New York Herald, Saturday, April 15, 1865, p.1,
col. 4, lines 28-30.

was on Booth's escape route, it seems only natural that
Booth headed for the doctor's home to receive first aid.
Mudd may have been merely an unfortunate victim by his
apparent innocent acquaintanceship with Booth. The
doctor received a life sentence for giving aid and comfort
to Booth. Several years after the trial, Mudd was par-
doned for his heroic medical deeds performed while he
served time in a federal prison. Mudd escaped the death
penalty because the court never proved that he was guilty
of being an accomplice in the crime. Consider the following facts in favor of the physician:

    a) He was a doctor sworn by oath to give aid to
       the injured.

    b) There is considerable doubt that Mudd knew of
       the shooting at Ford's Theatre when Booth
       approached him for treatment. Lack of rapid
       communication plus the fact that Mudd treated
       Booth only hours after the crime had been
       committed open serious doubts as to Mudd's
       knowledge of what Booth had done.

    c) Booth certainly did not intend to injure him-
       self at Ford's Theatre. He would have no
       reason, therefore, to include Dr. Mudd among
       his accomplices. Booth's arrival at Mudd's
       home for first aid may have been nothing more
       than a coincidence.

Mrs. Surrat's sacrifice

Booth and his confederates who actually wielded
pistol and dagger as they attacked government officials
marked for death along with Lincoln were obviously
guilty. Yet, history has not clearly established the
degree of guilt or innocence of any of the people who
went on trial and who in some cases forfeited their

freedom or their lives. For example, Dr. Mudd may have
been guilty only of knowing Booth. Mary Surrat may have
been found guilty because she had a son who was an active
southern courier and because she operated a boardinghouse
where Booth sometimes visited her son and other men found
guilty of the crime.

> The trial of Mrs. Surrat, first woman to
> be legally executed in the United States,
> provoked unending controversy. Many held
> her to be innocent, few believed her degree
> of guilt warranted hanging, but the verdict
> remained unchanged.[17] 9.22

A case of mistaken identity

Perhaps the most intriguing and mystifying aspect
of the trial concerned the establishment of the identity of
John Wilkes Booth from a photograph. Witnesses to the
shooting were asked to identify the photograph as that
of the murderer--John Wilkes Booth. This they failed
to do simply because all through the trial the photograph exhibited was that of John's brother Edwin, also
a famous actor and equally as well known as John.

> Yet, the photograph /of Edwin 7went un-
> 7.23 noticed into the files of the trial and
> history has failed to record this slip--one
> of the most tragic mistakes in American
> jurisprudence.[18]

5.26 •

Of all the mysteries and problems arising

9.43 [17]Kelly, The Crime, p. 31.
[18]Eisenschiml, Lincoln Murdered, pp. 264-65.

out of Lincoln's assassination, the enigma of
how Edwin's picture came to be substituted for
that of his brother John Wilkes is one of the
most intriguing.[19]

Booth's diary and the thirteen missing pages

Let us now turn our attention from the trial to the
diary kept by Booth. He had developed a habit of
recording interesting events of the day in a small blank
book.[20] After he was killed by federal troops (some
historians say he took his own life rather than be cap-
tured), the diary was discovered on his body and turned
over to the officer in charge. The diary eventually
found its way to the Secretary of War after having been
officially listed among the personal effects found on
Booth's body. Each of the pages in the diary was counted
and numbered. The officer called this to Stanton's attention when the diary was transferred to the Secretary's
care. However, when the diary was produced at the trial,
thirteen sequential pages in the middle of the book had
been torn out from the binding and were missing. The officer
in charge of the federal troops stated emphatically at the
court of investigation that the pages were all accounted
for when the diary was given to the Secretary. Stanton,
on the other hand, insisted that the pages were torn
from the diary before it was placed in his hands. It

8.20 [19]Ibid., p. 265.

[20]Frederick A. Morse, "The Trial of the Lincoln Assassins, A Probable Usurpation of Civil Justice"
(M.A. Thesis, The Graduate School of Cornell University,
1933), pp. 65-66.

was a case of one man's word against another man's word.
Stanton, being the superior officer, convinced the court
that the pages were missing when he received the diary.

Why has this diary been referred to so many times
by historians? Of what importance was it? Why did the
colonel or Stanton lie about the missing pages? According to the colonel who claimed that he had read the
diary, the missing pages offered incriminating evidence
implicating men holding government office in Washington.
Although no office holder was mentioned by name, the iden-
tification of these individuals was eagerly sought after
by the investigating officers and the court of inquiry
but to no avail. Booth, the man who wrote the entries
in the diary, was shot and killed before he could be
questioned. Throughout the following years, historians
have searched diligently for clues leading to the identity
of the persons left nameless in Booth's diary.

Was Stanton implicated?

One name that keeps coming to the attention of
historians is that of Edwin M. Stanton, Secretary of War
during Lincoln's administration. It is the opinion of
Eisenschiml,[21] Bishop,[22] Sandburg,[23] and writers who

9.24   [21]Eisenschiml, Lincoln Murdered, pp. 434-35.
        [22]James Alonzo Bishop, The Day Lincoln Was Shot
(New York: Harper & Brothers, 1955), p. 257.
        [23]Carl Sandburg, The Prairie Years and the War Years
(New York: Harcourt, Brace and Company, 1954), p. 723.

have documented the assassination that Stanton, a pol-
itically ambitious man and an outspoken critic of the
President, acted in a very peculiar manner following the
slaying. For example, why did he keep the name of the
assassin a secret until three hours after the crime, knowing that every minute's delay reduced the chances for
apprehending the criminal? No one has been able to explain Stanton's motives for withholding the name of the
murderer when it was an established fact that the culprit
was John Wilkes Booth.

Consider also how Stanton reacted to the news
brought to him by the chief of detectives, General
LaFayette C. Baker. Baker reported to Stanton, "We have
got Booth." Stanton said nothing in return but waited
a full minute in silence and then left the room without
a word.[24] This was strange behavior for a man who should
have been overjoyed at the news that the manhunt had
been successful.

An interesting story of a coded message prepared by
General Baker shortly before his death alleges that
Stanton helped plot the murder of Lincoln.[25]

Time erases evidence

It is tragic that each passing year washes away

---

[24] Eisenschiml, Lincoln Murdered, p. 150.

[25] Robert H. Fowler, ed., "Was Stanton Behind
Lincoln's Murder?", Civil War Times, 3, August-
September 1961, p. 5.

another bit of evidence concerning the Lincoln murder.
Interpretations by different writers do not always agree.
In fact, the many different accounts serve to muddle the
affair even more than it already is. If one wishes to
judge Stanton on circumstantial evidence, then the finger
of suspicion points heavily at him. However, this is not
the American way to determine the guilt or innocence of
individuals.

Perhaps more would be known about the conspirators
in the killing of President Lincoln if the son of this
great man had not destroyed many of his father's personal
papers. In 1925, a year before his death, Robert Todd
Lincoln burned some of his father's unpublished papers.
He gave as his reason that he saw no useful way in which
the evidence contained in the letters and manuscripts
could be used. He further stated that the incident and
all connected with it were long since dead and he did not
wish to reopen the case. Robert Lincoln never elaborated
upon his comments and in so doing added more mysteries
to those that already surrounded the murder. We can only
conjecture as to the contents of the burned papers.[26]

It is almost a certainty that the motives for killing the President, the mysteries surrounding the event,
the identity of the conspirators, and the actions of individuals close to the President will never be fully known.

---

[26]Emanuel Hertz, The Hidden Lincoln (New York:
The Viking Press, 1938), Preface.

4.11

9.51   9.53

7.38

BIBLIOGRAPHY

Bishop, James Alonzo. The Day Lincoln Was Shot. New
9.55   York: Harper & Brothers, 1955. 9.27

Current, Richard N. Mr. Lincoln. New York: Dodd, Mead
9.54   and Co., 1957.

8.6 Eisenschiml, Otto. Why Was Lincoln Murdered? New York:
     Grossett and Dunlap, 1937.

Fowler, Robert H., ed., "Was Stanton Behind Lincoln's Murder?"
     Civil War Times, 3, August-September, 1961.

Hertz, Emanuel. The Hidden Lincoln. New York: The
     Viking Press, 1938.

Kelly, Edward James. The Crime at Ford's Theatre.
     Washington, DC: Government Service, Inc., Action Pub-
     lishers, 1944.

Morse, Frederick A. "The Trial of the Lincoln Assassins,
     A Probable Usurpation of Civil Justice."
     M.A. Thesis, The Graduate School of Cornell
     University, Ithaca, New York, 1933.

New York Herald, Saturday, April 15, 1865.

Sandburg, Carl. The Prairie Years and the War Years.
     New York: Harcourt, Brace and Company, 1954.

U.S. Department of the Interior. Lincoln Museum and the
     House Where Lincoln Died. Booklet, reprint. Washington,
     DC: Government Printing Office, 1956.

The World Book Encyclopedia, 1982 ed. S.v. "Lincoln."

TERM PAPER CHECKLIST

		Yes	No

1. Does my introductory paragraph get the paper off to a flying start? _____ _____
2. Does the introductory section state specifically the purpose of my paper? _____ _____
3. Have I developed the body of the paper according to the outline? _____ _____
4. Does each paragraph link up with the previous and following paragraphs? _____ _____
5. Does each paragraph have one central thought? _____ _____
6. Are the lengths of my sentences varied to avoid monotony? _____ _____
7. Have I refrained from drawing too much material from one source? _____ _____
8. Does the language sound like my own? _____ _____
9. Have I eliminated meanderings and unnecessary repetitions? _____ _____
10. Does the paper accomplish my objective as stated in the opening paragraph? _____ _____
11. Do my conclusions rest on the evidence presented in the paper? _____ _____
12. Do all comments of my own stem from my findings? _____ _____
13. As I read it over, is my paper clear, does it make sense? _____ _____
14. Is it interesting to read?
15. Does the paper reflect my best effort? _____ _____
16. Is my paper's physical presentation neat and attractive? _____ _____
17. Is it grammatically free from errors? _____ _____
18. Have I proofread the paper to double-check spelling and punctuation? _____ _____

continued on next page

Yes   *No*

19. Are the pages, except page 1, numbered in the upper right-hand corner in the correct order?

20. Have I checked the accuracy of my quoted material?

21. Are short quotations of three or four lines or less enclosed in quotation marks and run in with the contextual matter?

22. Are longer quotations indented and set off in single-spaced type with no quotation marks?

23. Does each quotation carry a footnote reference?

24. Is the bibliography in correct form?

25. Is one method of numbering footnotes used consistently throughout the paper?

26. Have I double-checked the accuracy of these footnotes?

27. Is every source mentioned in a footnote included in the bibliography?

Each of the above questions should be answered with a "Yes." If you have answered with a "No," check that particular aspect of your term paper because you have done something wrong.

ABBREVIATIONS COMMONLY USED
IN REFERENCE BOOKS

A.D.	after the birth of Christ (*Anno Domini*, in the year of our Lord)
ad loc.	at the passage cited (*ad locum*, to or at the place)
aet.	aged
anon.	anonymous
ante	before
app.	appendix
art.	article
b.	born
B.C.	before Christ
bibliog.	bibliography
bk.	book
bull.	bulletin
C. or ©	copyright
ca.	about (*circa*)
cf.	compare
cf. ante	compare above
cf. post	compare below
chap.	chapter
col.	column
comp.	compiled, -er
Cong.	Congress
d.	died
DAI	Dissertation Abstracts International
diss.	dissertation
div.	division
ed.	edited, -or
ed. cit.	the edition cited
e.g.	for example (*exempli gratia*)
encyc.	encyclopedia
enl.	enlarged
esp.	especially
et al.	and others (*et alii*)
etc.	and so forth (*et cetera*)
et passim	here and there

et seq.	and the following (*et sequens*)
ex.	example
f.	following page
fac.	facsimile
fasc.	fascicle
ff.	and the following pages
fig.	figure
fl.	flourished, greatest development or influence
fn.	footnote
fol.	folio
front.	frontispiece
hist.	history, -ical, -ian
ibid.	in the same place (*ibidem*)
id. or idem	that same person
i.e.	that is (*id est*)
illus.	illustrated, -tion
infra.	below
in re	about
introd.	introduction, -ed
jour.	journal
l.	line
lang.	language
loc. cit.	in the place cited (*loco citato*)
MS. (MSS.)	manuscript(s)
narr.	narrated by
n.b.	note well (*nota bene*)
n.d.	no date
n.n.	no name
no publ.	no publisher
n.p.	no place given for publication
n.s.	new series
numb.	numbered
op. cit.	in the work cited (*opere citato*)
o.s.	old series
p.	page
par.	paragraph
passim	here and there
per se	by itself, of itself
pl.	plate
post	after
pp.	pages
pp. 2ff.	page 2 and the following page

pref.	preface
Ps.	Psalm
pseud.	pseudonym
pt.	part
pub.	published, -ication
q.v.	which see, whom see (*quantum vis; quode vide*)
r. or recto	right-hand page of a book
rev.	revised
sc.	scene
scil.	to wit (*scilicet*)
sec.	section
ser.	series
sic	thus
sig.	signature
st.	stanza
supp.	supplement
supra	above
s.v.	under the word or heading (*sub verbo*)
trans.	translated, -or, -ion
v., vide	see
v. or verso	left-hand page of a book
vide ante	see the preceding
vide infra	see below or the following
vide supra	see above
viz.	namely (*videlicet*)
vol.	volume
v.s.	see above (*vide supra*)
vs.	against

INDEX

Abbreviations
  common, pp. 119–21
  unusual, 5.8
Author reference in
  bibliography, 4.12 a–z
  card catalog, 3.30–.32
  footnotes, 8.24–.25

Bibliography (Chapter 4)
  citations, 4.11
  common types, 4.12 a–z
  computer-produced, 3.11
  content, 9.52
  final, 4.2, 4.12
  form, 9.54–.55
  location, 9.51
  number of references, 4.4
  preliminary, 3.27, 4.8
  sample. *See* sample term
    paper, p. 116
  typing. *See* Typing the
    paper
  working, 4.1, 4.3, 4.5–.6,
    4.12, 5.1

Cards
  analytic, 3.35
  author, 3.30–.32, 3.35
  card catalog, 3.28–.34
  Dewey Decimal System,
    3.36 a
  Library of Congress
    System, 3.32, 3.36 b

note cards, 3.26, 5.5–9,
  6.3. *See also*
  Notetaking
"See," 3.34
"See also," 3.34
subject, 3.31, 3.35
title, 3.30–.31, 3.35

Footnoting (Chapter 8)
  common types, 8.25 a–z
  formal style, 8.2–.3, 8.8
  Latin, use of, 8.19–.24
  purpose, 8.1, 8.5–.6
  simplified style, 8.2–.3, 8.8
  typing. *See* Typing the
    paper, footnotes

Ibid., 8.19–.20, 8.24
  in sample term paper,
    pp. 6, 8, 12
Idem, 8.19, 8.23–.24

Library, using the (Chap-
  ter 3)
  abstracts, 3.44 b, c, f–j, m–
    o, q, u, v
  almanacs, 3.44 r, 3.45
  atlases, 3.46
  audio-visual equipment,
    3.21

automation, 3.17
books "on reverse," 3.3
carrels, 3.22
Circulation or Loan
    Department, 3.4
computer printout, 3.25
computer-produced
    bibliography, 3.11–.14
computer search, 3.12–.14
Database, 3.11–.12, 3.14
    Biological Abstracts,
        3.11
    ERIC, 3.11, 3.15 a–e,
        3.44 f
    MEDLARS, 3.11
    Psychological Abstracts,
        3.11
Dial Access, 3.20
dictionaries, 3.27, 3.44 a–f,
    i–k, m, p–t, v, 3.47
divisional reading rooms,
    3.9
encyclopedias, 3.27, 3.44
    a–f, h–m, p–u, 3.45–.46
ERIC, 3.11, 3.15 a–e,
    3.44 f
    *Current Indexes to
        Journals in Education,*
        3.15 c, 3.44 f
    descriptors, 3.15 e
    Document Résumé,
        3.15 d, e
    Research in Education,
        3.44 f
    Resources in Education,
        3.15 b, 3.44 f
    *Thesaurus of ERIC
        Descriptors,* 3.15 a,
        3.44 f

Guide to Reference Books,
    3.42
information retrieval, 3.11
Interlibrary loan service,
    3.10
microcard, 3.16
microform, 3.16, 3.48
microprint, 3.16, 3.48
newspaper indexes, 3.37,
    3.41

Periodicals Department, 3.8
Physically disabled users,
    3.50

*Readers' Guide to
    Periodical Literature,*
    3.38–.39
Reading Room, 3.5
Reference Librarian, 3.6,
    3.19
Reference Room, 3.7
rotary files, 3.24, 3.28
Special Collections, 3.23
Special reference books and
    indexes, 3.44 a–v
accounting, banking,
    business, economics,
    finance, 3.44 a
agriculture, biology,
    chemistry, medicine,
    3.44 b
anthropology, 3.44 c
art, music, 3.44 d
biography, 3.44 e
education, 3.44 f
energy and the
    environment, 3.44 g

engineering, science,
technology, 3.44 h
folklore, mythology,
3.44 n
geology, geography,
3.44 i
history, 3.44 j
language, acronyms,
synonyms, proverbs,
quotations, 3.44 k
literature, 3.44 l
mathematics, physics,
3.44 m
nations, political science,
3.44 o
philosophy, 3.44 p
psychology, 3.44 q
radio, television, 3.44 r
recreation, sports, 3.44 s
religion, 3.44 t
social science, 3.44 u
United States, public
documents, 3.44 v
vertical files, 3.28
Xerox, 3.18
yearbooks, 3.44 e–f, u,
3.45
Loc. cit., 8.19, 8.21, 8.24

Notetaking (Chapter 5)
brackets, use of, 5.27
how to take, 5.2–.18
index cards, use of, 3.26,
5.5–.10
safeguarding, 5.2, 5.29,
7.41–.42
types, 5.11–.14, .17
using with outline, 6.3–.4,
7.12

Op. cit., 8.19, 8.22, 8.24
Oral reports (Chapter 10)
appearance during
presentation,
10.77–.80
attitude toward, 10.64
audience analysis, 10.20,
10.94, 10.102
audience fatigue,
10.101–.102, 10.108
audience rapport,
10.81–.83
communications skills,
importance of, 10.1–.3
contingency plan, 10.95
data gathering, 10.21–.26
determining equipment
needs, 10.67–.68
differences between term
paper and oral report,
10.4
editing the draft, 10.40,
10.51, 10.55–.56
establishing target dates,
10.18
evaluating the presentation,
10.117–.122
getting started, 10.17–.18
giving the presentation,
10.84–.102, 10.108
handout materials,
10.109–.110
how much to know about
topic, 10.16, 10.96
jokes and funny stories,
10.103–.107
language. *See* under
Writing the paper
length of talk, 10.99–.101

note cards, 10.21–.26
opening and closing the
    talk, 10.30–.32
Oral Report Checklist, pp.
    95–98
paragraph headings, 10.39
preparing audiovisuals and
    demonstrations,
    10.69–.76
preparing the outline,
    10.27–.28
purpose, 10.6–.8
questions, 10.102,
    10.111–.116
    direct, 10.102
    indirect, 10.102
reading the speech or using
    note cards, 10.59–.63
rehearsing the oral report,
    10.5, 10.58, 10.61,
    10.64–.65
room arrangements, 10.66
shortening or lengthening
    the talk, 10.50
speed of delivery, 10.49
staying within time
    allowance, 10.100
systems chart for
    completing assignment,
    10.19
taping the final copy,
    10.48–.58
three parts to a speech,
    10.29
topic, selection of,
    10.10– 15
    controversial type, 10.14,
    10.96

noncontroversial type,
    10.13
typing the draft or final
    copy, 10.41–.47
voice quality, 10.5,
    10.53–.56, 10.84–.85
why give a speech, 10.6–.8
why speeches fail, 10.9
writing the draft,
    10.33–.39. *See also*
    Writing the paper
Outline, making the (Chap-
    ter 6)
    divisions within, 6.9
    main headings, 6.9–.12
    numbering, 6.9–.10
    order, chronological, 6.6
    order, time occurrence, 6.5
    preparing from cards,
    6.3–.4
    relationship to note cards,
    6.3
    revising, 6.7
    sentence form, 6.13
    topic form, 6.13

Presentation. *See* Oral reports
Public Speaking. *See* Oral
    reports

Speech. *See* Oral reports
Subjects, choosing and
    limiting the (Chap-
    ter 2)
    for oral report, 10.10–.15
    for term paper, Chapter 2,
    pp. 6–11

Talk. *See* Oral reports
Term paper (Chapter 1)
  checklist, pp. 117–18
  description, pp. 3–4
  importance of, p. 2
  sample, pp. 99–116
  See also Typing the paper;
    Writing the paper
Typing the paper (Chapter 9)
  bibliography form, 4.11,
    4.12 a–z, 9.27,
    9.51–.55. *See also*
    sample term paper,
    p. 116
  carbon copy, 9.10
  cleaning typewriter, 9.14
  completed paper, 7.38
  cover, 9.18
  folder, 9.2, 9.17, 9.58
  footnotes
    accuracy, 9.44
    common types, 8.25 a–z
    numbers, 8.9, 8.12–.13,
      9.43, 9.45
    punctuation, 8.7
    space allowance, 7.18,
      8.18, 9.19, 9.26, 9.46
    spacing, 8.15
    typing, 8.14, 9.54
    underscoring, 8.16–.17,
      9.24–.25, 9.30–.31
  general appearance of
    completed paper,
    9.4–.9, 9.13–.14
  margins, 9.17–.18, 9.20,
    9.28
  outline, 9.36–.38
  page numbers, 9.39
  paper slection, 9.3, 9.29

  paragraphs, 7.28, 9.42,
    9.47, 10.39
  proofreading, 9.56
  quotations, 5.21–.25
    brackets, use of, 5.27
    copying, 5.22–.23
    ellipses, 5.24–.26
    error within quotation,
      5.28
    laws and formulas, 5.21
    long, 7.23, 9.22–.23
    poetry, 9.48
    punctuation, 9.50
    within quoted matter,
      9.49
  spacing, 9.21–.22, 9.27
  tables, 7.44–.52
  title, 9.34, 9.40–.41
  title page, 9.33, 9.35. *See*
    also sample term
    paper, p. 100
  type size, 9.15–.16
  typewriter ribbon, 9.13

Writing the paper (Chap-
    ter 7)
  carbon copy, 7.16, 9.10
  coherence, 7.32
  consistency of footnotes
    and bibliographic
    entries, 7.35
  documentation, 5.19–.20,
    7.19–.20
  draft copy, 7.17
  editing, 7.34–.37
  error in reference, 5.28
  final draft, 7.34, 7.36–.38,
    9.7

first draft, 7.5–.37
handwritten copy, 9.5–.6, 9.8
ink color, 9.6
instructor's copy, 7.16
language, 10.33–.38, 10.40
   action verbs, 10.33
   adjectives, 10.36
   adverbs, 10.36
   colloquial and slang
     expressions, 7.8
   grammar, 7.6, 10.37
   passive verbs, 10.34
   personal references, 7.10
   sentence structure, 10.35
   unnecessary words, 10.38

word choice, 7.9
notes, 7.7
number of words, 7.2
opening and closing
   paragraphs, 7.4, 10.32
paper, 7.15, 9.3–.5
paragraph design, 7.27–.30,
   9.42
quotations, 5.22–.27,
   7.21–.25
   long, 9.22–.23
   short, 7.21
superscript, 7.26
title, 2.4, 7.3

Notes

Notes

Notes

Notes

Notes